The Hypochondriac's Bedside Book

by Les Karamazov

The
Hypochondriac's
Bedside Book
by
Les Karamazov

M
PAPERMAC

First published 1987 by
PAPERMAC
a division of Macmillan Publishers Limited
4 Little Essex Street London WC2R 3LF
and Basingstoke

Associated companies in Auckland, Delhi, Dublin, Gaborone, Hamburg, Harare, Hong Kong, Johannesburg, Kuala Lumpur, Lagos, Manzini, Melbourne, Mexico City, Nairobi, New York, Singapore and Tokyo

ISBN 0-333-44949-5

Reprinted 1987

Typeset by Emerald Graphics Limited
Printed in Great Britain by Richard Clay plc, Bungay, Suffolk

Edited by Richard McBrien
Design by Matt Black

Thanks to Ken Ellis, ex-doctor and male model

BIOGRAPHY

Les Karamazov has been at least seriously ill for most of his life. A confirmed worrier since birth, he spends his free time worrying about such things as Life, Meaning and whether he will run out of things to worry about.

As a medical student Les Karamazov quickly discovered his ability to catch virtually any disease simply by reading about it. Over the course of his six year training he was hospitalised for more than fifteen months, often baffling some of the finest medical minds in the country with his bizarre combination of symptoms.

Since these early successes Professor Karamov has gone on to dedicate his life to the study and practice of Hypochondria. Often sneered at, rarely taken seriously, he has persevered with his researches, discovering and suffering from many important and hitherto unknown diseases. In this new work he brings together his years of experience and misery in the hope that Hypochondriacs everywhere can break new ground.

Les Karamazov lives in K Wing of Beckonworth Hospital with his third wife, Hilary, an anaesthetist.

HOW TO READ THIS BOOK

As with most things in life there is a right and a wrong way to read this book. The wrong way is to bite it and then hurl it out of the window. The right way is to wash your hands, hold it open, worry about bending the spine, shut it, examine it, wash it, open it carefully, read a page, worry about the back cover, shut it, read the back cover, wash your hands, open it, realise it's upside down, shut it, turn it round, open it and drop it on your foot. If you fail to follow these instructions you will impair your satisfaction and will not be able to worry as much as you might wish – and may catch a nasty disease.

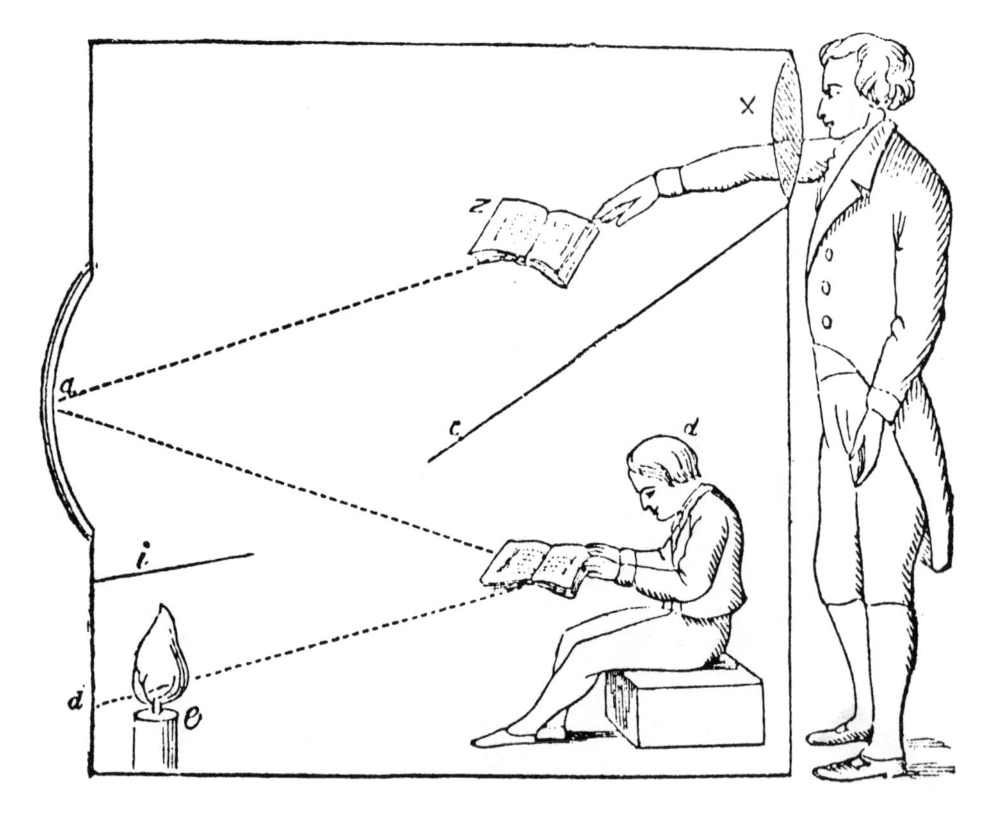

PREFACE

I have known the author of this exciting new volume since we were at school together. Since then our paths have taken very different routes – his to the very heights of the Himalayas and mine to a career in Government.

However, during all the many years that I have known him we have always kept up our correspondence, and indeed I feel that I have almost climbed some of those exciting peaks with Charles.

It was, therefore, with great pleasure, that I agreed to lend my name to a Preface to this book in the humble hope that it might encourage a new generation of butterfly lovers to scale new peaks and climb new paths on mountains everywhere.

All I can do is to wish Charles Heliotrope, and his wife Hetti, the very best of luck with this project and hope that 'The Diurnal Lepidopterist's Mountain Song Book' will soon climb to the top of the bestseller lists.

Major Richard 'Red' Admiral

HOW MUCH OF A HYPOCHONDRIAC ARE YOU?

Before reading this book it is important to establish just how much of a hypochondriac you are. Therefore please answer the following questionnaire:

1. **You wake up with a crick in your neck. Do you:**

   a) Hope it will go away.
   b) Assume you slept badly because of something you ate.
   c) *Know* it is the onset of cancer.

2. **You are going to dinner with some friends. Do you:**

   a) Take them a bottle of wine.
   b) Ring beforehand and tell them you are allergic to spinach.
   c) Take along a stomach-pump just in case.

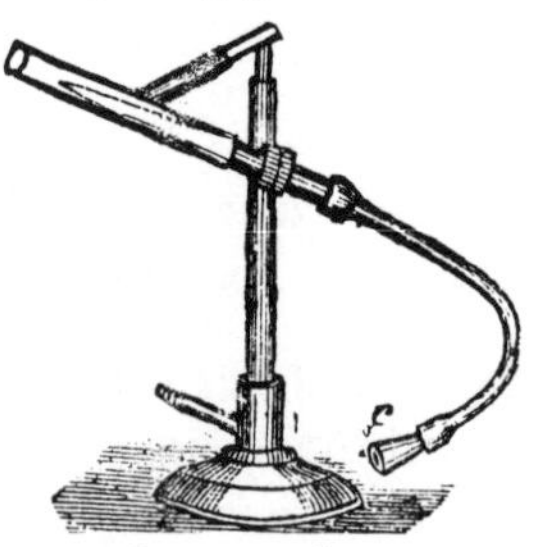

3. **You have met the partner of your dreams and are about to seduce him. Do you:**

   a) Whisper sweet nothings in his ear.
   b) Take a bath.
   c) Get him to have a bath and administer a series of blood tests.

4. **You are in a crowded lift when it suddenly stops. Do you:**

   a) Tell everyone to keep calm.
   b) Tell everyone about your agoraphobia.
   c) Die.

Answers

If you answered mostly a) you are living in a fantasy world and have no idea how dangerous every-day life can be. Read this book.

If you answered mostly b) you are not quite as blind as the above but could still improve your awareness of life's dangers. Read this book.

If you answered c) you are a true hypochondriac. Go to bed immediately, take lots of liquid and ring your doctor.

SMOKING

Smoking is one of the major problems of our times - much bigger than drug addiction or alcoholism. It is probably connected to a host of serious medical ailments. Yet millions and millions of people seem unable to kick the habit. Why?

The answer is that one of the ingredients of tobacco, nicotine, is a highly addictive drug - almost quicker acting than heroin. Cigarette companies rely on people trying cigarettes and getting 'hooked'.

WHAT ARE THE SYMPTOMS?
A quick rule of thumb is: clouds of smoke.

IS IT SERIOUS?
Especially if there are flames too.

IS THERE A CURE?
A large number of cures have been tried - ranging from hypnosis to nicotine flavoured chewing gum. Recent advances in treatments have produced very encouraging results using one of the following methods:

a) Giving the patient exploding cigarettes.
b) Inserting the cigarette into the patient's mouth hot end first.
c) Setting fire to the patient's hair.
d) Chopping off the patient's fingers.
e) Beheading the patient.

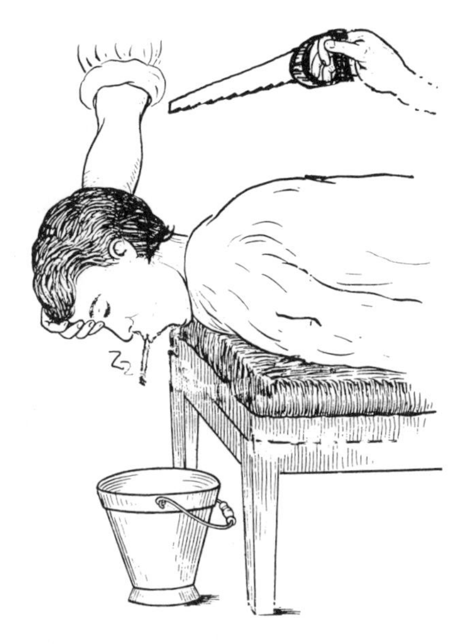

DIARY OF A HYPOCHONDRIAC

Wednesday 10th SEPTEMBER

3.00am	Wake up - worry that world has ended. Check body for buboes. Wash hands.
4.00am	Wake up - still breathing so assume world okay. Wash hands.
5.00am	Wake up - throbbing pain - fear appendicitis. Call doctor.
6.00am	Finish talking to doctor - tells me appendicitis occurs only in abdomen not behind ear.
6.10am	Throbbing pain moves to abdomen.
6.12am	Called doctor - phone seems out of order.
9.00am	Wash hands and disinfect mouth. Noticed left small toe is smaller than the others - suspect shrinking. Measured all important parts of body - worried - left arm seems bigger - Expanding Disease?
10.00am	Get up. Too ill to work - take day off. Wash hands. Sterilise breakfast cereal. Find mould on bread.
10.30am	Regain consciousness.
11.00am	Take rectal temperature - nearly lose thermometer.
12.00pm	Exhausted – time off to worry.
4.00pm	Wash hands. Notice swelling on face - call doctor.
4.05pm	Doctor says noses are normal - make note to change doctor.
5.00pm	Do exercises - breathless - Miner's Lung?
6.00pm	Anti-septic bath - skin reacts badly - apply moisturizer.
7.00pm	Moisturizer causes heat rash. Take pink pills.
8.00pm	Feel dizzy. Check Medical Dictionary - seem to have M-L inclusive.
9.00pm	Wash hands. Retire to bed - too ill to eat.
12.00am	Throbbing pain moves to knee - brain tumour?

SPOTS

Spots are probably the most worrying thing adolescents have to deal with - that and the thought of never losing their virginity. Indeed, most people think the two are contingent - how can you lose your virginity if you haven't first lost your spots? Speaking as a Doctor it is my responsibility to assure young people that spots are not as bad as they seem. Acne always seems worse to the sufferer and, in time, will pass. Speaking as a human being I can only say Ugh - I wouldn't touch a spotty person with a bargepole.

There are two approaches to dealing with acute acne - treatment and camouflage.

Treatment - the spot must be removed from the surface of the skin. Suitable tools for this include: pumice, sand paper, electric plane, blow torch.

Camouflage - disguising the pimple is a temporary though effective measure, relieving the sufferer from embarrassment.

FLYING

Airline companies have conspired to convince us that if you propel a chunk of metal fast enough through the air it will in fact stay up. Hypochondriacs are not, of course, so easily fooled. It is self-evident to the worrier that no aeroplane can stay up for very long. It simply is not natural - heavy pieces of machinery do not fly through the air.

Problems with flying start long before the plane takes off. Indeed before you even see it. The airline suggests you arrive a mere two hours before take-off, but any proper worrier will realise this is cutting it absurdly fine - a good three or four hours is much more like it. This allows for typical delays such as burst appendix, gall stones or small earthquake.

Once in the airport enough time has to be left for losing tickets, passport and children, as well, of course, as the occasional terrorist incident. Deciding what to check-in and what to carry on can be highly traumatic. What if the plane should crash into a mountain range and you were left only with your one under-the-seat bag? How would you cope without a spare set of underwear? Should you take an extra book along to pass the time? What is your moral position on cannibalism? Will you need the Teach Yourself book on Ethics to help you out?

Choosing the correct seat is not to be taken lightly either. Only a fool would sit near the front of the plane - the first ten rows wouldn't stand a chance if it nose-dived. On the other hand any bombs will probably be in the hold and blow the back half off. Seats near the wings might seem the best bet, but these are disturbingly close to the engines and fuel tanks. While an aisle seat gives quick access to the gangway, the best emergency exits are over the wings. Undoubtedly the worst position is a middle seat, although a terrorist is less likely to choose his victim from here and, if you keep really quiet and make an effort not to look American, European or Middle Eastern, he might not notice you at all.

Dress for flying brings its own worries. Bundling up against the English cold can make you appear a complete idiot when you arrive in Barbados. But what if you are re-routed via Alaska and are forced to spend a freezing cold night in Anchorage? And of course you never know who you might be sitting next to. While sweat pants are comfortable they won't further your career if you're sitting next to the French Ambassador.

The emergency procedures the hostesses go through are hopelessly inadequate and intended for the average traveller who has no more concern for his own life than he does for his free easi-wipe towel. The serious worrier will politely ask the hostess to go through the routine in slow motion, and insist that they try on the life-jacket - who's to say that someone hasn't walked off with it in Karachi as a memento? Even if it's still there it could have a puncture - bring your own repair kit.

Airline food should only be eaten with great caution. If it is infected you might be the only person on the plane who remains calm and collected - the lives of over 300 people could depend on you not eating the paté. On the other hand, if the plane is forced to land on an uninhabited island, the paté might be your last food for several days. The wise traveller will therefore carefully pack the entire food tray into his overnight bag for just such an eventuality.

PROLONGED EXPOSURE

It is a favourite saying of the non-hypochondriac that x or y is 'perfectly harmless'. However, there is now overwhelming evidence that prolonged exposure to apparently safe things can have alarming side-effects.

Man who has watched 'The Price is Right' over a period of two years.

THE WRONG DIAGNOSIS

SYMPTOM: *Stiff Joints*

FIRST DIAGNOSIS: *Might be Rheumatism or Arthritis; might be lack of exercise.*

REAL PROBLEM: Acute case of calcification, the patient was experiencing premature *petrification.*

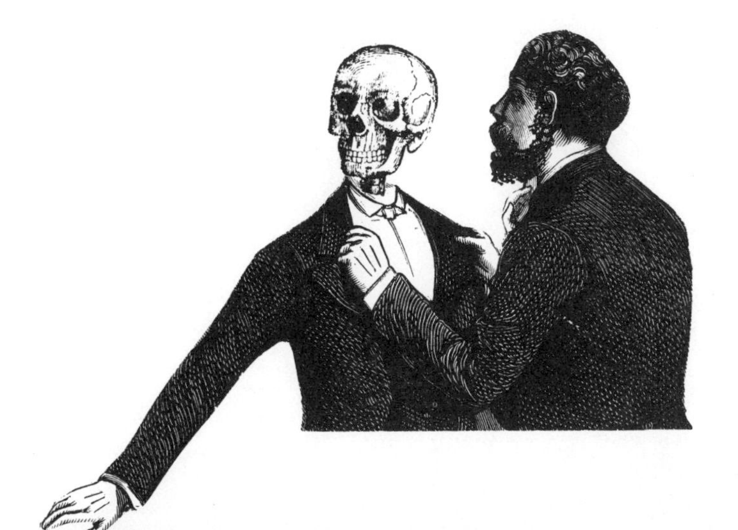

DEPRESSION

In everybody's life there will be moments of depression. I, for example, remember I was particularly depressed in 1936 when I lost a yellow marble down a drain. If you have not been depressed, or feel you are not getting your fair share of this very trendy disease, simply ask yourself a few questions:

Do I have the best job in the world?

Am I happier/more successful/wealthier than all my friends?

Have I made a major contribution to human civilisation this week?

Am I deeply in love with someone who deeply loves me?

If the answer to any of these is no, then you have ample reason to be depressed.

The medical profession has a number of very effective ways to combat depression. The most common is to administer anti-depressants - these cause the patient to rise up to the ceiling and float around for a few hours - it is difficult to be depressed when upside down.

Another, perhaps less effective, treatment is the 'talking-to', which can be administered free of charge by mothers, relatives and friends, or for £50 an hour from a therapist. This usually consists of the simple message, 'Brace up, things could be worse' which, as a dedicated Hypochondriac, you know to be true.

BALDNESS

A lot of people worry about hair - that they've got too much of it or too little. Many men think they are unattractive when bald - I can honestly say that this is indeed so. Women simply do not find baldness sexually attractive. In the same way men do not find excessively hairy women a turn-on. So what to do if you are a little thin on top - well, you could try finding a hairy women, or, short of that spend a great deal of money at a Harley Street clinic getting hair around your body - study the diagrams below when choosing what to move where.

AGENT'S SYNDROME

Description: After birth, buying a house is probably the most traumatic experience you will ever go through. It is attended by a number of afflictions, the most common of which is Estate-Agentitis. Allergic reaction to Estate Agents is found in 99% of the population (the other 1% ARE estate agents, and even some of these are allergic to themselves). To understand the complaint better we need to examine the life-cycle of the virus, Agentigazumper.

Symptoms: Estate Agents are parasites that live off the house buying community by sucking their blood and emptying their bank accounts. They make contact with the host through carefully constructed traps offering wonderful new homes for knock-down prices. Indeed so friendly do they seem that most victims make the first approach themselves, attracted by the bright lights and cosy atmosphere of the agent's lair, or office as it is known.

It is only once the parasite has lulled its victim into a state of ease, usually with cups of coffee and promises of finding a three bedroomed house with garden for £10,000, that its true nature emerges. Early symptoms include sending the victims to totally unsuitable houses that bear no relation to the printed details, or tempting them with bargains just out of their price range.

After an incubation period of some months the victim finally chooses a new house and the Agent enters its second, more advanced stage - indeed this is the busiest time for the parasite as it makes re-newed effort to sell the house to somebody else at a higher price, tells the vendors they can get more and pretends to the buyers that all is well. In this way the truly professional Agent can boost the house price, and therefore its profit, several times within a month, leaving its victims physically and mentally exhausted. When the deal finally goes through the parasite has still not finished with its hosts, but continues to bombard them with offers of larger, better and cheaper houses while pointing out what a killing could be made on the one they've just bought.

Treatment: At present there is no known cure for Agentitis, although there is a certain satisfaction to be had signing up for all possible mailing lists when you are not even contemplating buying. This wastes the Agent's resources, but of course it will simply extract more from its victims the next time round to compensate. The only long term solution is to become a nomad.

CULTUREUM or BRAGG'S DISEASE

Description: Reading books you don't understand, going to unintelligble plays, sitting through incomprehensible films, watching Albanian operas and pretending you enjoy them all.

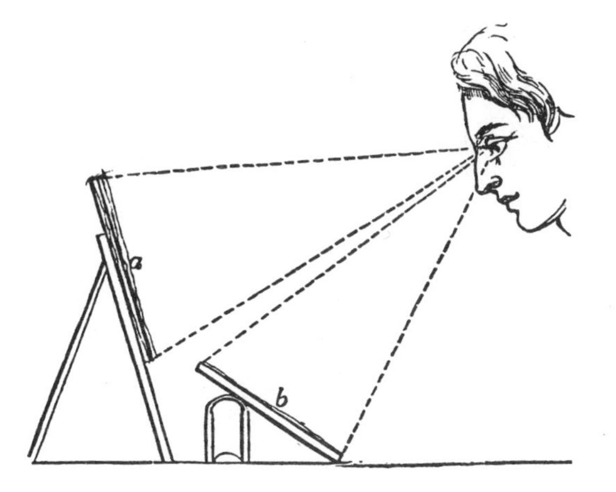

Symptoms: Usually breaks out in fashionable bars, cafes and restaurants. Compulsive repetition of certain stock phrases in a loud voice, with disregard for what anyone else is saying and continual straining of neck to see if anyone important has just walked in. Phrases to note include: "The semiological motive of Man/Nature/Car was evocative of his earlier work." "I really enjoyed the use of space and the sense of movement." "Conceptually it's a throwback to Auerbach's techniques."

Treatment: The aim of all treatment must be to get the patient to admit enjoying something simple, understandable and above all not trendy. To this end it is best to place the patient in homely surroundings with no Perrier or copies of Blitz in sight. Start with Disney films (which still have Cultureum traits) and move on through Tom and Jerry to pop music, comics and finally "Terry and June". However, if the patient admits liking this the process has gone too far and a dose of Cubism should be administered immediately.

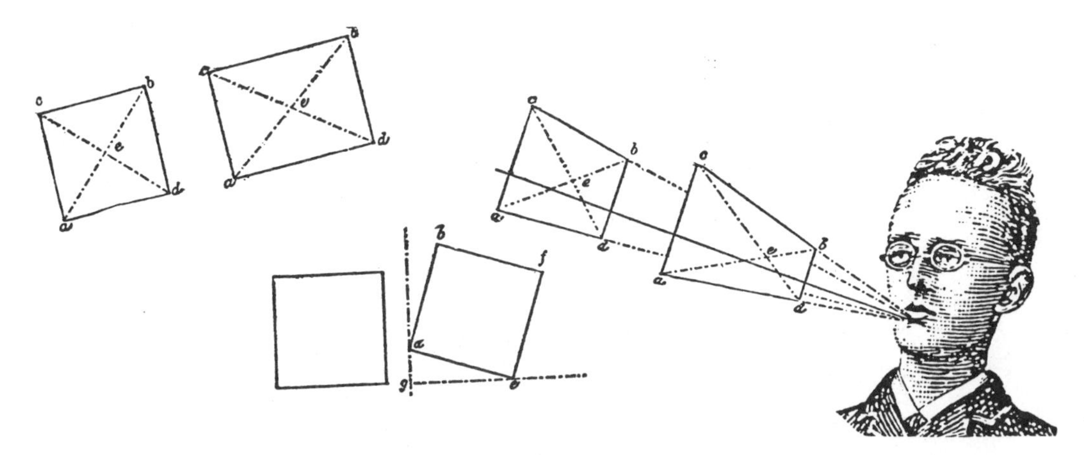

SELF-EXAMINATION

When you wake up in the morning you will not have seen your body for at least eight hours, so run this quick body check.

1. Have any pieces dropped off in the night?
2. Have any new pieces appeared?
3. Are all the pieces in the same place?

Once you have checked these basics you can move on to a more detailed examination. Some areas are more difficult to check than others, the small of the back for example or behind the ears. To overcome this here is a simple to use device to help you see hidden parts.

IN AN EMERGENCY

Some questions to ask yourself:

1. *Am I still alive?*
2. *Am I breathing? If yes, beware any toxic fumes in the vicinity. If no, see under Death - the ultimate worry.*
3. *Can I see? If no, how come you can read this? Perhaps you have not gone blind but are suffering from Lying Disease.*
4. *Are all my limbs still attached to me?*
5. *Can I feel anything?*

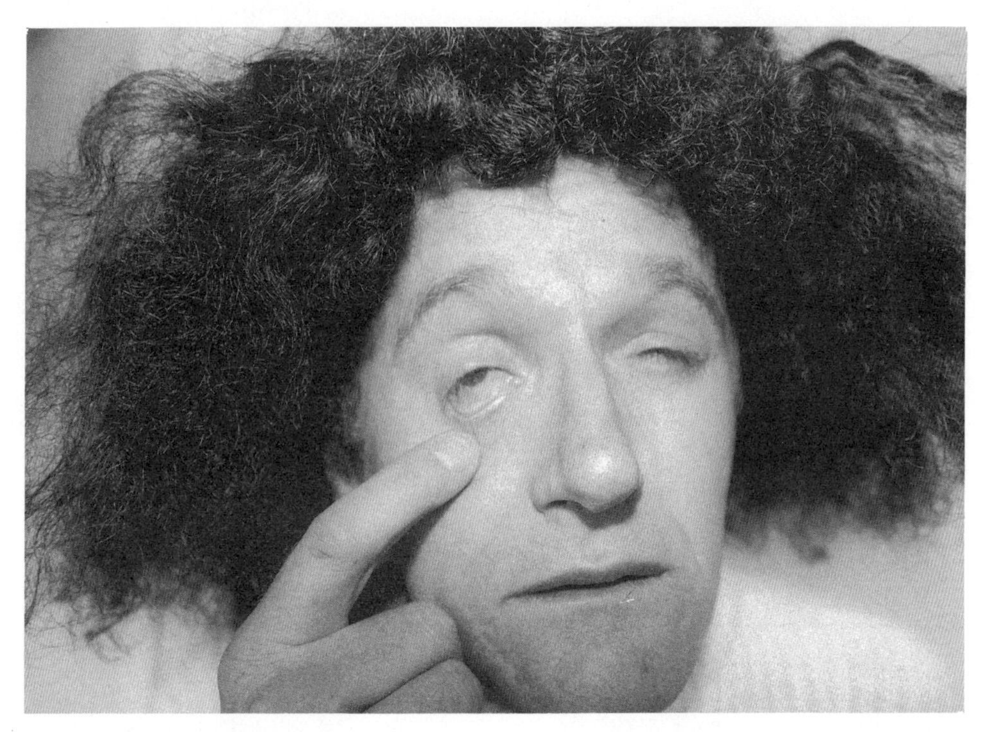

Eyes – check to see if you can see them.

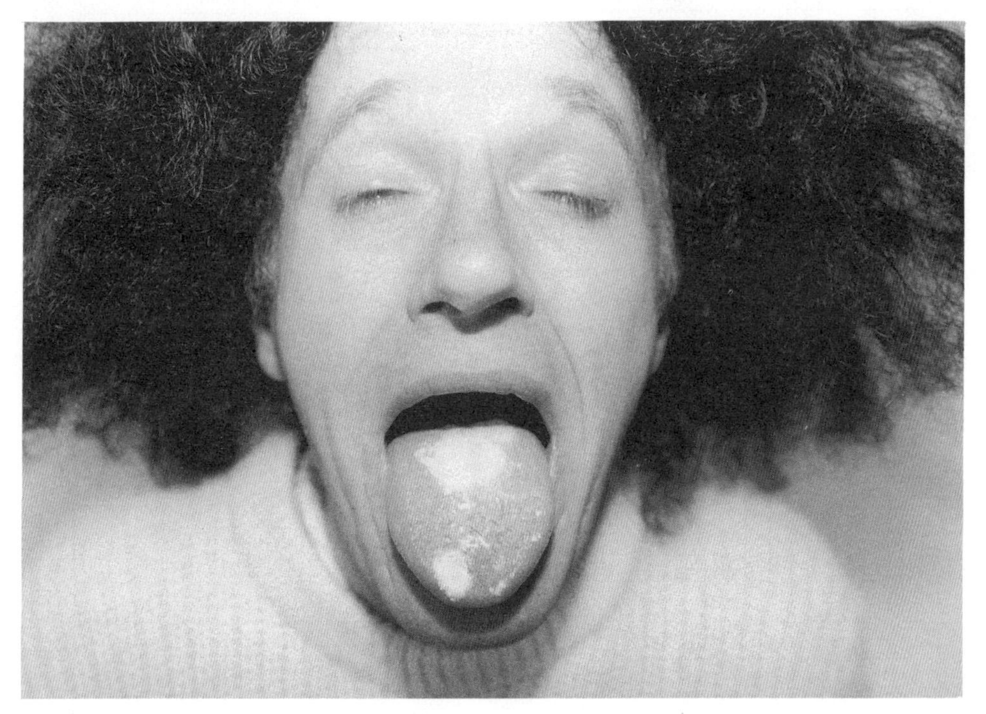

Tongue – this should be wet and pink – it should not be frothing, textured or have hieroglyphics on it.

FORMS

As a hypochondriac it is essential to assess the risk of infection at any given moment. However, it can be acutely embarrassing to ask personal questions of people you hardly know. I have therefore devised a series of forms for every occasion. Simply hand these to people you suspect of harbouring germs and say you work for a market research company.

Potential lover
Have you slept with any of the following in the last ten years:
Goats
Men
Women
Kebabs (please indicate rare or medium)
Did you wash afterwards?
Have you got any broken skin on your body?
How many running sores did you have at the last count?
Do you touch during intercourse?

Taxi Driver
When did you last disinfect the back seat?
Is there any epilepsy in your family?
What was the age, sex and medical history of the last three passengers?
When did you pass your driving test?
How many accidents have you had in the last year?

Waiter
Would you mind if I saw your finger nails?
Are there any illnesses in your family?
Is there a toilet in the restaurant?
Does it flush?
When did you last use it?
Did you wash your hands afterwards?
When was the last time you had a bath?

IS MY BRAIN WORKING?

A common worry of middle-aged men is that they are not getting their point across and failing to make sense. This problem consists of suddenly thinking you are not making car parts in Chicago meat packers. Nine times out of ten the affliction is imaginary, others do not notice that you are a yoghurt with small feet. However, if you do feel the condition coming about the best thing is to go for a wink and try to eat the watch I bought for Christmas. Alternatively you can record your voice and see if it makes a lampshade for the sitting room.

CLOTHES

Twenty four percent of all non road accident deaths are caused by people wearing wrong clothes! Staggering isn't it? Yet how many give their wardrobe a second thought when it comes to keeping disease at bay?

I know people who will wrap up when it gets cold outside but they do this only to keep warm, not to keep the 'bacteria at bay'. How many of them remember to tuck their vests into their underpants to stop venereal crabs, which might easily be blown from an open window down their back, taking root?

I have listed here a few ideas for sensible clothing, but they are only common sense and you will easily be able to improvise.

Starting at the bottom.

Shoes - always wear polythene bags over them and remove these and discard (without touching them of course) before going into a house. Only a madman would carry the filth of the street onto his carpets.

Socks/Stockings - antistatic silk are the best; tie a little aluminium foil to the top and trail it behind you to disperse static electricity.

Trousers - rubber bands round the ankles will stop scorpions and tarantulas from climbing up the legs; use only natural, undyed fabrics and have no rubber in contact with the body (carcinogenic).

Skirts - very risky garment; if they must be worn wear the Victorian style pantaloons beneath and treat as "trousers" above.

Underwear - there are sadly few shops that still sell padded, thorn proof, insect repellent, sanitised, support thermal underwear; however, if you can track them down your troubles will be over; otherwise you will have to fabricate this yourself; (Ladies - black lace trim can make these garments quite appealing).

Tops - anything with a buttoned neck and cuffs will do; beware unhygienic fabricators and soak all garments in disinfectant before wearing. All upper garments should have a quick release ripcord (for urgent removal) and should be pre-perforated for quick tearing into strips for slings, bandages, tourniquets etc.

Gloves - most essential in the wardrobe; line with rubber and do not remove until safely in bed.

Hats - You can really let your creativity go here; there is very little that can go wrong with hats, so be inventive! (do of course remember to wear a tight fitting rubber bathing cap beneath the motorcycle crash helmet you should wear at all times).

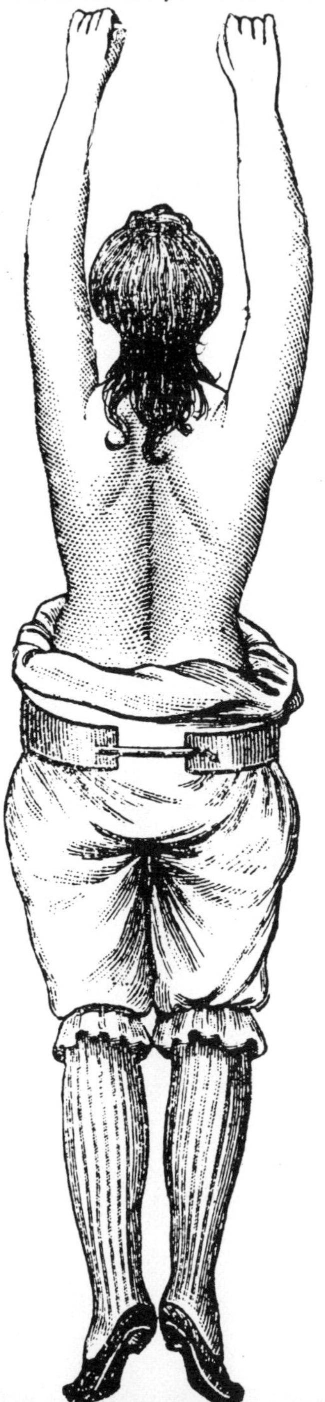

THE WRONG DIAGNOSIS

SYMPTOM: *Vomiting*

FIRST DIAGNOSIS: *Gastro-enteritis or mild food poisoning; if persists look out for problems with kidneys.*

REAL PROBLEM: Hypo-allergy; patient is *self-allergic* and the body is getting rid of itself.

HOMEOPATHY

The principle of Homeopathy is to treat the disease *with* the disease. In the case of worry this means finding a corresponding worry to combat the original one. The Homeopathic Worry Chart below gives the necessary counter worries.

Worry	**Counter-worry**
Nobody loves you	*They probably have good cause.*
You have a vast overdraft	*The financial system could crash tomorrow.*
Your wife has left you	*She could have gone off with your best friend.*
You're losing your looks	*Nobody has noticed.*
No chance of changing your awful job	*You might be fired next week.*
Life seems meaningless	*Everybody else knows the meaning except you.*

ACCIDENT BLACK SPOTS

(and how to avoid them)

Hand blow-driers

Increasingly these types of hand driers are found in public washrooms, ostensibly to promote hygiene, but sadly they are a menace to health. Severe damage can occur to the delicate bone structure in the palm of the hand when the large ON button is pressed. This bruising may be further aggravated by infection from the bacteria that the previous user left on the button.

New Clothes

Are your clothes REALLY new? Just because they come packed in layers of cellophane does not mean that your 'new' clothes have not been worn before. Most shops allow people to try on before buying and even exchange clothes afterwards. Shop assistants become pretty deft at wrapping them up again.

Imagine! Your clothes may have been worn by dozens of other people each one with diphtheria. The answer of course is to hang around at the back of the store and check when the new deliveries are made, race round the front and watch as the garments are hung out.

PEOPLE

People are by their nature unhygienic and therefore best avoided. It is far better to mix with inanimate objects as they are less likely to carry disease and have a longer attention span. Small rocks make ideal theatre companions while cutlery is inconspicuous at a dinner table. 18th century side-tables can be receptive and of course a sofa is always welcoming after a hard day's work.

However, if you feel you must be with people, it is essential to find someone compatible; not all complaints get on well together – athletes foot and dandruff often bicker while gall bladder and prostate trouble seem to make for a stable relationship.

Finding someone with complementary diseases can be a lifetime's work but carefully worded advertisements in the more obscure medical journals can achieve results:

> Sincere asthmatic seeks double by-pass for ongoing side-effects. Medical record appreciated. Genuinely ill only please.

Here are some other ways of making contact – simply follow the instructions below and gauge their reaction:

1. Wheeze in their ear.
2. Comment on the resurgence of Lassa Fever in Nigeria.
3. Ask to examine their handkerchief.
4. Casually drop your stool sample.

5. Take their pulse.
6. Place all your pill bottles on the table.
7. Ask them to hold a bottle while you fix up a drip.
8. Show them your X-rays.

DINEREUM

Description: An ancient affliction consisting of being forced to eat a meal with people you'd rather see participating in a Japanese TV game show.

Symptoms: There are several strains.

1. **Bore** - see Boritis.

2. **Slide Syndrome** - two hours of last year's holiday slides, usually accompanied by such riveting commentary as 'That's Henry outside the hotel - it's a bit blurred but he's the one wearing the sombrero.'

3. **Gameosis** - here the hosts insist that everybody reverts to a mental age of five and play charades, pass the parcel and, in extreme cases, murder in the dark. Can lead to adultery, marital break-up and smashed china.

4. Comatosis - one is expected to drink so much that unconsciousness sets in before midnight. Bringing up the lasagne over the stairs is considered a good sign, as is attempting to drive home when three times over the limit.

5. Pairoffs Disease - this is invariably transmitted by a host who places you next to someone of the opposite sex with whom you have nothing in common except a strong desire to be somewhere else. Despite discreet hints that you find them physically repugnant and intellectually dormant, your host will insist on telling you all about each other and then urge you to tell your story about the time you lost your watch in Crete. Once the dinner party has started it is almost impossible to extricate yourself - short of passing out in the soufflé you are simply going to have to groan and bear it.

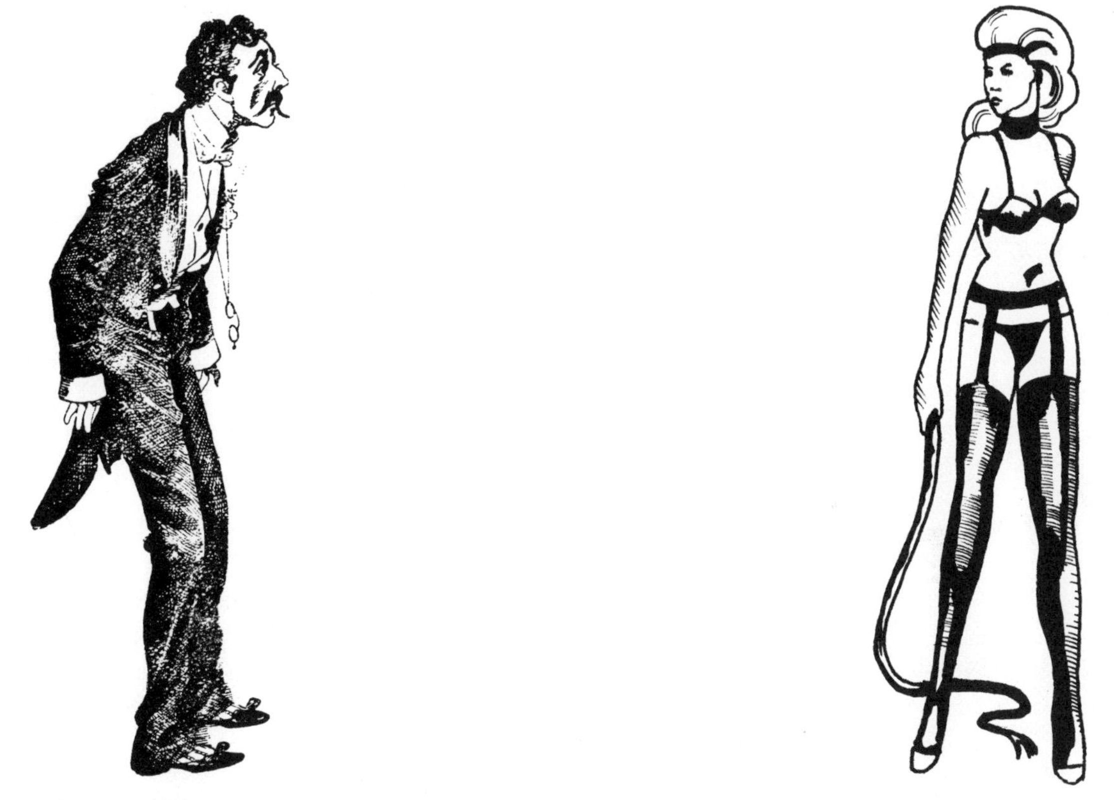

6. Cordon Bleuphy - the onset of this disease can be quite pleasant - the victim is invited to sample the product of the host's latest series of night classes. However, the effects can stay with you for several days and after tasting 'L'assemble de Turd' you might wish they had studied history of art instead.

7. Pontificatum - one member of the party launches, at great length, into what is wrong with the county/country/world and how he could easily solve all Man's problems given the chance and a spare Saturday afternoon.

Treatment: Refuse all dinner invitations.

CARDIAC ARREST

This is one of the commonest diseases that affects the more affluent classes. It usually strikes in the early morning, very often as the victim is sitting at the breakfast table opening the mail.

What Happens?
The victim will let the opened envelope fall, go white and start gasping for breath. Shortly after, he or she will start shouting at his or her spouse or children. Unmarried victims often call the police and complain of someone stealing their wallets.

What Types of Cardiac Arrest Are There?
Some of them are domestic. Barclay's Syndrome and Restricted Access, and some have been carried here, probably on cargo vessels, such as Diner's Lumpy Throat and American Excess.

Does It Get Better With Time?
Not really; once the trouble has started you only have thirty days or so to clear it up.

What Do I Do?
Really, surgery is the only way to cure the problem once and for all, though some people try and spin things out with other methods.

When Surgery Is Necessary

The operation is not a major one and can be performed under a local anaesthetic with a pair of scissors. Simply grip the offending cardiac and cut it swiftly in half. The pain will be sharp momentarily, but disappears soon. Beware relapses and watch for danger signs, however innocent they may at first seem, such as a craving for Phonecards and even *in extremis* Kidney Donorcards.

HICCUPS

Hiccups are nothing to laugh at – each year several million people die of hiccuping and many more are unable to leave their front rooms. A hiccup is in fact a respiratory *stigmata* – and nobody would think it was funny if you couldn't breathe.

The old wives' tales of drinking a glass of water backwards or having a kilo of ice put down your back tend to belittle what can develop into a very serious complaint. Hiccuping is one of the first signs of drowning – produced by a reflex action in the *meta-thorax* which produces the sudden rasping, gasping sound. This 'drowning out of water' is not as uncommon as might at first be thought and it is wise to take precautions against it, such as carrying a snorkel, if you are prone to hiccups.

HICOUGHS

This malaise, commonly confused with Hiccups, is in fact completely different from it except for the similarity in pronunciation, though in its way also worrying. Hicoughs are spasmodic cough type noises that come from down in the second stomach. They are produced by the action of excess acids there dissolving the wall of the liver and giving off carbon dioxide, which is emitted in these little 'coughs'. The best treatment is an antacid rubbed on the stomach.

EAR, NOSE AND THROAT

Ear, nose and throat, or ENT as we doctors call them, are often beset with tricky medical problems. The first thing to do when examining these parts of the body is to ascertain whether they are indeed present, only then can you move on to more sophisticated tests – such as are they in the right place, in the right numbers.

Existence

Nose – place an old piece of Camembert in front of your face, close your mouth and breath in. If you reel backwards and feel like throwing-up you probably do have a nose. If you smell nothing but quite fancy eating the cheese you are either French (for which there is no known cure) or have no nose – refer yourself to a specialist immediately. (If you are French *and* have no nose you could consider emigrating to Quebec.)

Ears – go into the garden at 3am and blow loudly on a trumpet. If you see people sticking their heads out of windows mouthing silently at you the chances are you do not have ears or are deaf (this is what the people are trying to tell you). If you can hear the insults loud and clear there is nothing wrong with your ears – though you might like to consider moving soon.

Position

It is not enough to simply have ears and a nose – they must be located in the correct place. Sit in front of a mirror and compare yourself to the diagrams below – if you do not look like either Diagram a) or b) do not panic – you are a freak and should have a promising career in travelling circuses.

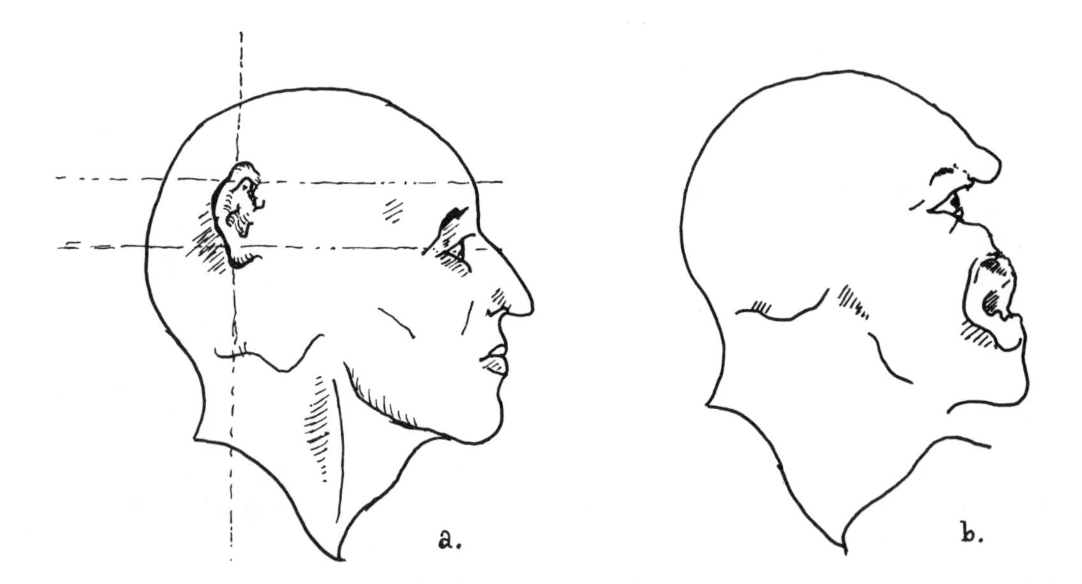

Care

The nose is very close to the brain. Do not therefore explore its inner workings too vigorously or you might end up pulling your brain out of your nostril – not only a social gaffe but extremely difficult to rectify since the brain does not function well when removed from the skull. There are correct and incorrect ways of picking – as the following diagrams demonstrate:

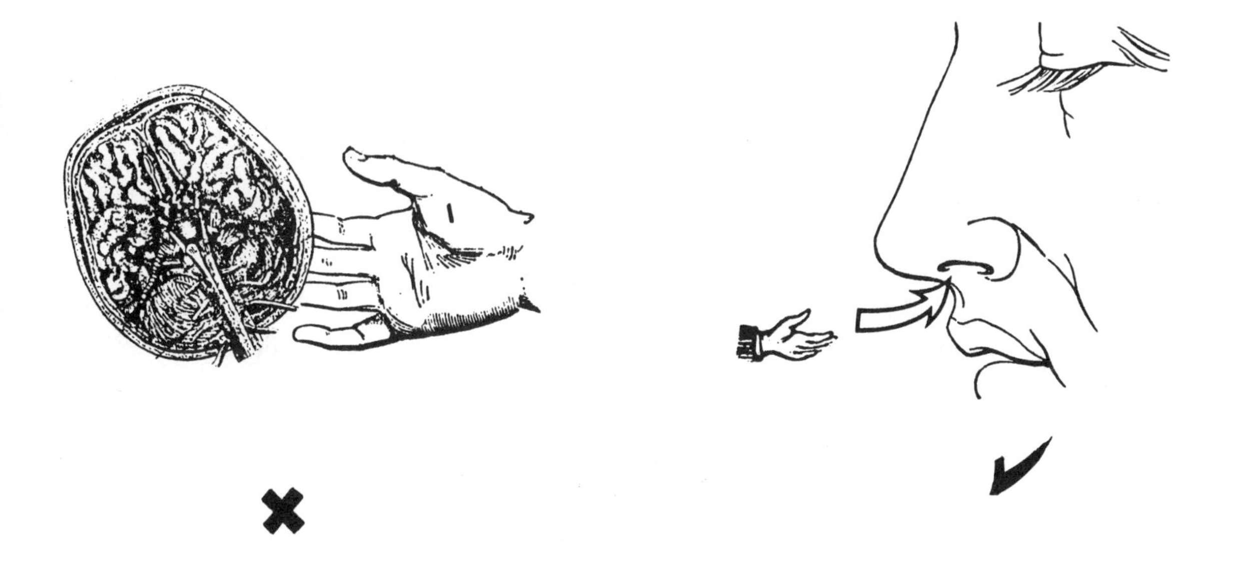

IS MY BRAIN WORKING ?

Pre-senile dementia afflicts 100% of the adult population at some time or other. The symptoms are temporary but indicative of troubles to come.

The first signs are losing ball-point pens or pencils and/or mixing up the names of the subject's children. The patient may recover temporarily then, or may sink further by either 'Writing Lists Of Important Things' or 'Forgetting Birthdays'. Hospitalisation may be needed when this latter turns out to be the patient's own birthday.

The chemical process that goes on in the brain is not exactly known but there seems to be a desire in the patient to live in the past. A feeling that time is passing very quickly occurs, and if asked suddenly to name a record in the Top Ten the patient may very well mumble inaudibly.

Is There Anything To Be Done?
Bed early, not too much excitement, plenty of gardening, knitting, hot chocolate and watching the news on TV seems to be what most sufferers like.

HYGIENE

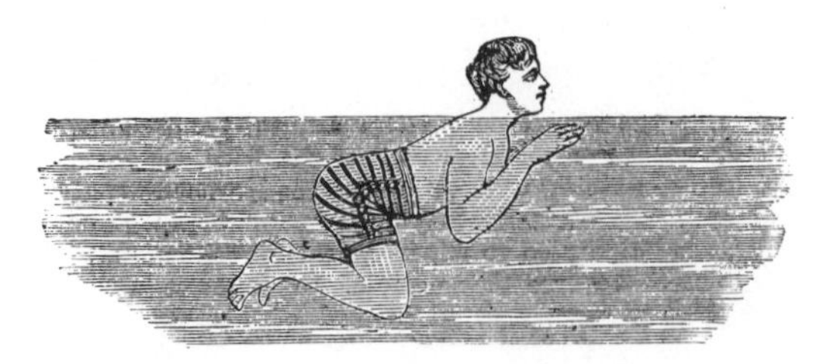

Washing

While on the surface washing may seem an all-round 'good thing' hypochondriacs know that it is riddled with dangers. Too much washing removes the body's natural oils, dries out the skin and may cause the body to shed its outer layer like a snake. On the other hand greasy, smelly people rarely do well at parties.

The actual process of washing therefore has to be gone through with considerable attention.

1. Decide on a bath or a shower. Baths are really just another way of bathing in your own dirt. Showers, on the other hand, never seem able to get into those hidden nooks and crannies – unless you do a handstand (see Gymnastics).

2. Adjust the temperature of the water – too hot and you'll open your pores so much vital organs could slip out, too cold and your skin closes down for the duration, trapping dirt forever.

3. Pick your soap. Soaps now come in a wide variety of cancer-causing forms. The safest are probably those with the least smell and plain wrappers – but who wants to go around smelling like a public lavatory? 'Special' soaps include Japanese granules, which is the equivalent of a rub down with sandpaper, and 'medicated gels' which kill off all harmful bacteria but also remove essential lubricants, stretching the skin so tight on your face you go round with a permanent grin.

4. Carefully wet the body, taking care not to swallow water as this causes death.

5. Lather the soap and spread all over the body – but do not be too energetic as it can be difficult to extract small bars of soap from some areas – and more difficult to explain how they got there.

6. Rinse off all traces of suds – again, taking care not to drown.

7. Rub dry with a towel. Coloured towels can run, impregnating your now vulnerable skin with toxic dyes guaranteed to cause leukaemia - so choose the soft white variety, taking care not to rub too hard - you don't want to knock any bits off.

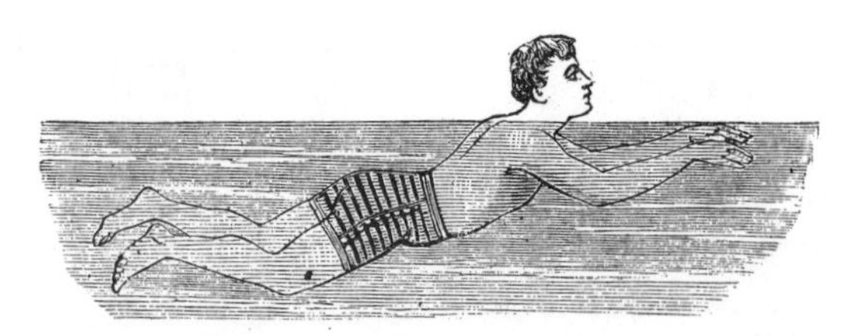

Shaving

Shaving is as complex as washing and should not be undertaken lightly. If in any doubt – grow a beard (but do see HAIR AND ITS DRAWBACKS). If you must shave, follow these guidelines:

1. Wet face – see above for danger of drowning.

2. Lather the face with soap. Aerosols are not recommended since they not only damage the ozone layer, thus causing devastating climatic changes, but can explode with the force of anti-personnel mines if overheated.

3. Pick up razor and scrape face carefully. This is the most hazardous part of the operation – the smallest slip can result in cutting your own throat – not only messy but it will definitely make you late for work. The golden rule is – open your eyes.

4. Wash soap off face and pat dry with sterilised towel.

THE WRONG DIAGNOSIS

SYMPTOM: *Runny Nose*

FIRST DIAGNOSIS: *Catarrh; possibly allergic reaction, or mild 'flu'.*

REAL PROBLEM: Unstemmed loss of white blood corpuscles due to an internal blockage in the pancreas (where the corpuscles are made); if the blockage is not cleared death will result due to loss of the corpuscles; in emergency block up nose with tissues to keep them in the body.

NATURE'S CURES

How many times a day do you hear the words 'Mother Nature Knows Best'? Quite a few I should think; well you do in my consulting rooms anyway. Many doctors today are beginning to believe that we have overlooked some of the natural remedies that our forefathers used, often with startling results.

All sorts of illnesses *malignus non-existens* can be cured by using the right herb, potion, or plant.

It can be really quite difficult getting kids, and indeed the whole family, to take the right medicines or eat healthy food. The advantage of the following little titbits are that they are not only nature's medicine but also quite tasty in their own right when you get used to them. Prepare your family for a healthy treat.

Viper's Bugloss Ketchup
Kids will love this - the bright green colour is as tempting as the name and it will build up their immunity to St. Patrick's Dance.

Borage and Twig Egg Flip
A favourite with aunties, this flavoursome nightcap contains everything she'll need to ward off constipation.

Chervil and Dandelion Comfits
Excellent festive titbits that taste yummy and prevent Old Maids Kneecap.

Cold Anemone Soup
Another festive special that's easy to prepare in advance. The trick is to soak the anemones in goat's milk and leafmould for a week.

Horseradish Ice Cream
This one is a real surprise! Dad will love it and it will ward off Melancholic Baldness.

Mustard Roly Poly
A must for cold winter evenings, this hot and spicy dish is more liquid than the usual one, so it can be drunk. It is an ideal pick-me-up and prevents liverishness.

Bread and Borax Pudding
Despite its name this traditional dish is really quite tasty and after the initial surprise most people find it interesting; for inner cleanliness.

Ground elder Cookies
A lovely summer treat to have in the biscuit jar and it's nice to know that the family shouldn't suffer Crabtree's syndrome if they eat plenty.

Celandine and Bladderwort Crumble
No more wet beds with this one! A nursery favourite from yesteryear.

VITAMINS

The functioning of Vitamins is not generally understood by many doctors who still cling tenaciously to the *minimalist* theory on dosage and the *dismissive* theory on types. This is surprising when you consider that the Alphabet has been used for many, many centuries and most of these doctors know it by heart. Why do they then cling to the idea that small doses of only a few vitamins are necessary?

There are twenty-six letters in the alphabet and there are twenty-six Vitamins or Vital Mins as I call them. Not all chemists display all their Vitamins on their shelves, so it is important to ask for them by name, or rather Letter, and in reasonable quantity – about a kilo (4.5 pounds) a day per person per Vitamin is recommended.

A	good for skin problems; found in aluminium
B	good for teeth; found in yeast and dandelions
C	good for profits; found in America
D	helpful in combat situations; found in Chemists
E	improves sex life; found in beds
F	adds to enjoyment of Vitamins; found in Vitamin E
G	improves reading; found in books
H	synthesised from Queen Bee Jelly; helps flying
I	synthesised from Queen Bees; aids buzzing
J	extracted from Ginseng; helps Korean exports
K	keeps you regular; found in Bran packets
L	improves pharmacists; found in shops
M	makes hair shine; found in shampoo bottles
N	helps lists of Vitamins; never before noticed
O	good for nothing; not discovered yet
P	found in bottles; good for hypochondriacs
Q	good for headaches; found in aspirin
R	stops Vitamin deficiency; found on tongue tips
S	good for everything; found in Heaven
T	essential to make up lists of Vitamins; found here
U	found after T, above; good to come before V
V	good for filling in spaces; found in Vitamin lists
W	found three up from Z; found in just the right place
X	very good for some things; found here and there
Y	excellent in its place; very good when it is found
Z	phew; absolutely excellent when you get there

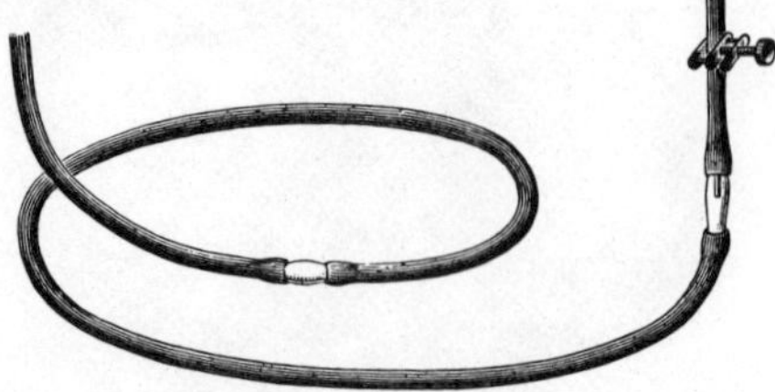

apparatus for administering

IS YOUR DOCTOR REALLY QUALIFIED?

Does your doctor look like this?

One in nineteen general practitioners, one in thirty five anaesthetists and a staggering one in seven surgeons are imposters.

Many people take it for granted that their doctor knows what he or she is talking about, that a doctor's word is gospel. But have you ever considered that your doctor could be a fraud? That he has hijacked a white coat and knows no more about illness and disease than a butcher - in fact he may well be a butcher.

Here are a few incisive questions to ask about doctors before you let them anywhere near you.

1. Can you read their writing? If you can they may be an impostor.

2. Do they have a tattoo saying 'I love Jeanne?' If yes, do not trust them.

3. When you enter the surgery do they say 'And what seems to be the problem?' or 'Watcha cock, what's up with you then?'

4. If you have a headache do they suggest aspirin and bed or major brain surgery?

5. Do they wear glasses? All real doctors wear glasses and look over the top of them.

6. If a man, does he wear a tweed jacket? If a woman has she a knee-length skirt? Any other clothing, such as ski pants or wet suits are incorrect.

7. Real doctors should precede references to all parts of the body by 'old' - 'what seems to be the trouble with the old waterworks/back passage/chest?' and NOT 'pisser/arsehole/bazookas'.

8. If they refer to your head as the bit above your shoulders, beware.

9. Do they talk to you for three minutes and prescribe some yellow pills or ask you a lot of questions about your health and run several tests?

ACCIDENT BLACK SPOTS

(and how to avoid them)

Being Sneezed At

It is very dangerous being sneezed at closer than twenty metres, and quite risky at anything up to a mile. The real risk is at the greater distances because you may not know it has happened and so cannot take evasive action (holding your breath till you get home).

I advise my patients to wear a hearing aid - even if they are not deaf. This will serve the dual purpose of magnifying the sound of the sneeze, so alerting you, and also close up one more body orifice to infection.

Drink Cans, with ring pulls

There seems to be a temptation for people to drink directly from a can of soda or beer. If you think about it, you do not know where this can has been so a few simple precautions are in order.

Before opening, examine the can for visible defects with a magnifying glass; if there are none immerse it in an ultrasonic cleaning bath and then without touching it immerse in a second bath of household disinfectant, followed by a quick spray of distilled water.

TELL-TALE THINGS TO WORRY ABOUT

Being overweight, or *Avoirdupois*, is a major cause of decreased life expectancy in the developed world; it is important therefore to make sure your weight stays at the correct level.

Causes

Eating too much; this in turn is caused by feeling hungry and so it is the hungry feeling that one has to tackle.

Succulent barbecued Cheeseburger
Crispy, savoury french fries
Avocado dip with corn chips
Warm cheese straws
Lobster cocktail
A plaster bust of Abraham Lincoln
Spaghetti carbonada
Chocolate fudge cake
Peaches, fresh raspberry sauce and cream
Caramel and almond doughnuts
Chocolate and marzipan pralines

If your eyes lingered longingly on the Plaster Bust of Abraham Lincoln then you are in full health. If not, depending on the length of time you spent thinking about the dishes, you are, to a greater or lesser extent suffering from *Avoirdupois*.

PILLS

The shape, size and colour of pills are good guides to their function. If your doctor fobs you off with 'just a little something to make you feel better' compare what he has given you with the chart below to see its true effect:

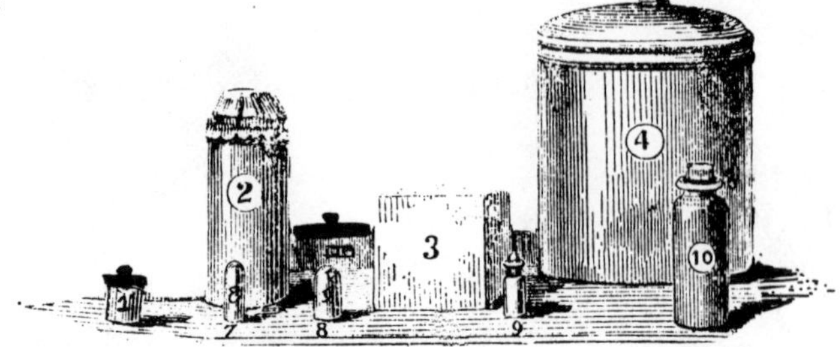

White Pills:
No need to worry much - in fact you can buy them yourself. They will be for something like bad breath, indigestion, headaches or calcium deficiency.

Larger White Pills:
Still no need to worry much - it could be just Vitamin C - unless you have to take more than one several times a day. In that case you could have something wrong with your heart or kidneys.

Very Little White Pills:
These can be quite serious - Scattica, Angelica and Thrombonist are likely problems especially if you have to take them after meals; however if you have to take them with meals or in tea then they are probably saccharine tablets.

Yellow Pills - any size:
These are the strongest in a physician's armoury. Yellow pills DO indicate that there is something quite seriously amiss. But don't worry - you are in good hands if you know a doctor who is able to prescribe yellow pills. If they have speckles of another colour in them, you have been given the VERY best.

Brown Pills - any size:
As you might expect, nothing remarkable is contained in these - routine medicine for bowel, hair or skin problems. But if you are not suffering from any of these and have a broken leg you might want a second opinion.

Red Pills:
Red pills are reserved for very serious cases - blood or brain problems, personality disorders, lungs and bone marrow deficiencies.

Size:
In general the smaller the pill the more serious the condition. Very large pills are probably not pills at all but should be taken rectally.

Shape:

Safe

Serious 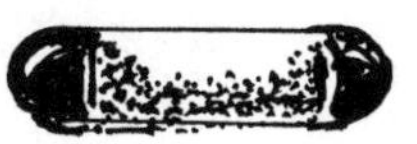

Harmless 

Could sell on blackmarket 

You've gone to the vet by mistake 

Other Points to Watch For:

a) If the tablet has a 'score' mark across its diameter, you can derate its importance by half.

b) Tablets or capsules in a blister pack roll are not serious drugs.

c) Pills or capsules in a plain white box mean there is something seriously wrong with you.

THE WRONG DIAGNOSIS

SYMPTOM: *Spots and Pimples*

FIRST DIAGNOSIS: *Adolescent hormonal problem or in adults poor diet.*

REAL PROBLEM: Worms; in the same way that garden worms leave worm casts of earth on the lawn, so parasitic worms in humans leave little mounds of mess on the face.

BITES AND STINGS

A good deal of ignorance surrounds the subject of bites and stings; many insects and animals are unfairly classified as venomous while others are dangerously ignored. Here is a list of biters and non-biters.

Things that do not bite

Flies
Woodlice
Phone books

Things that do

Bees
Wasps
Ants
Tigers (these can be very messy bites)
Waiters
Customs Officials

Treating Bites

Being bitten by a waiter is an increasingly common occurrence, especially in hot weather. A waiter's bite is marginally less dangerous than a customs official's but both should be treated seriously. The easiest remedy is to apply a tourniquet:

Mosquitoes

Mosquitoes carry a number of fatal diseases, including malaria and encephalitis. Many experts and tour operators claim that the problem has been eradicated in most holiday resorts and no precautions are necessary.

This is both a simplistic and dangerous attitude. It completely fails to take into account the capricious nature of the mosquito. There is no reason why an adventurous mosquito should not, one summer, take it into her head to visit Cannes or even Peckham. She may have had enough of the tropical clime and crowded air and decide to go somewhere quiet, cool and uncrowded. The hypochondriac is therefore advised to take anti-malarial pills throughout the year and wear a mosquito-net at all times.

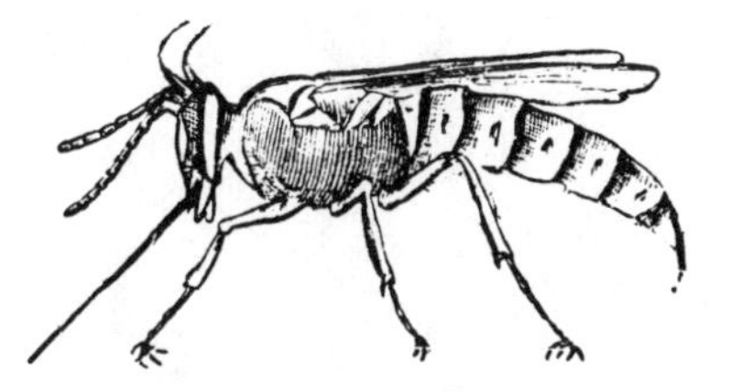

HOW TO READ YOUR MEDICAL REPORT

Most doctors are extremely selfish and keep medical records to themselves. This is probably a breach of the Hypochondriac Oath and, in the interests of your own health, you should make sure you obtain a copy of anything written about you.

When you have it, it may be a little jargon ridden; use these examples to help you decipher it.

"This patient is a time-waster" = this patient is suffering from terminal cancer but I don't have the heart to tell him.

"No signs of physiological difficulties" = unknown, fatal disease.

"Small increase in temperature" = high fever.

"Needs to relax a bit" = six months to live.

"An interesting case" = rare tropical disease.

"Refer to psychiatrist" = to prepare him for the worst.

"Ask for social worker to visit" = to arrange funeral.

Bathrooms

Bathrooms, especially other people's, are of course dirty, unhygienic places. There are more diseases per square inch in a bathroom than in just about any other place except a hospital (hospital bathrooms are therefore to be avoided at all possible costs).

If you do have to use somebody else's bathroom this can involve a precarious and challenging journey around the bathroom in an attempt to keep clear of the germ-infested floor. The diagram below outlines how to tackle a particularly treacherous bathroom climb.

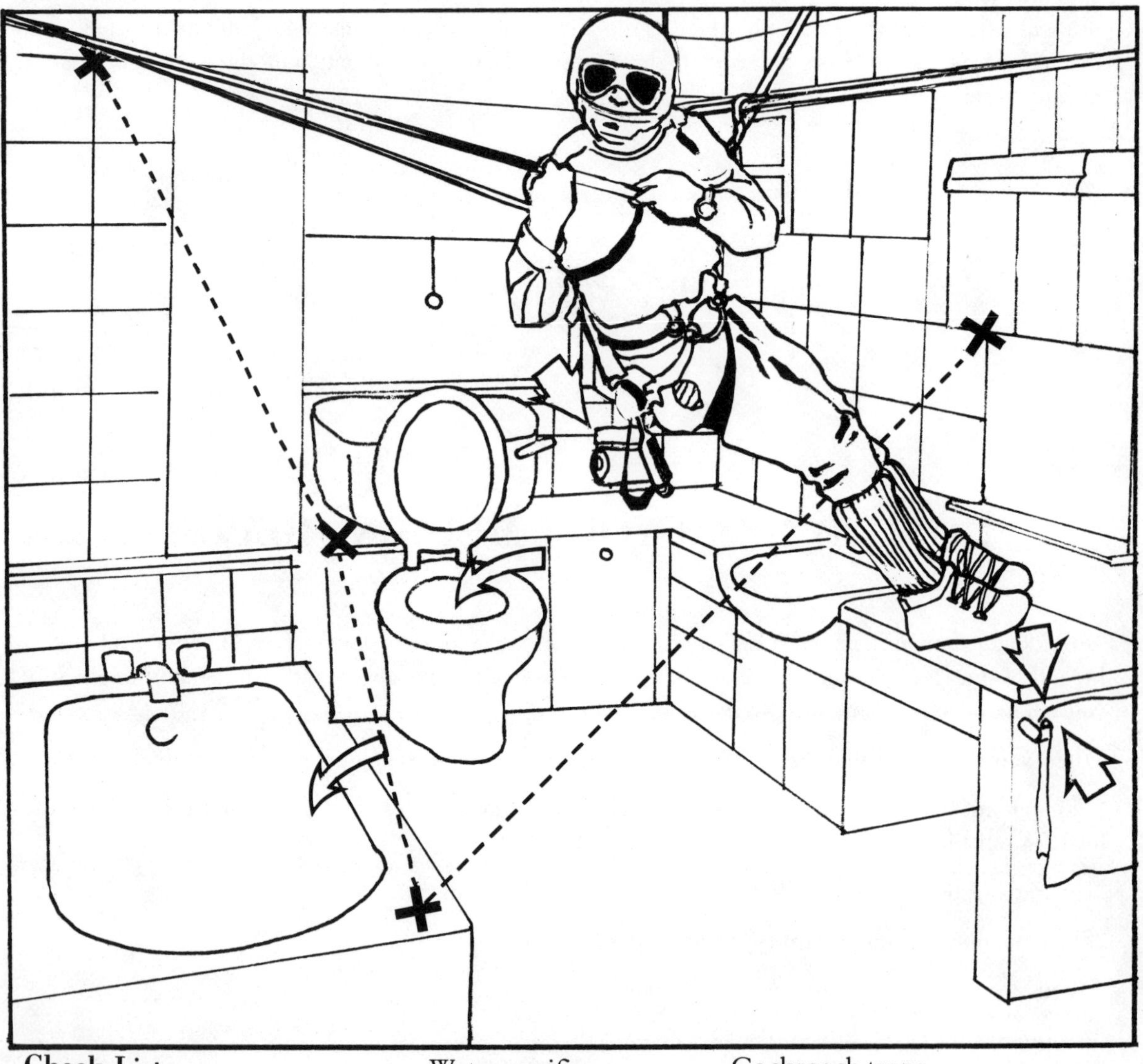

Check List
Polythene gloves
Plastic loo seat covers
Water purifier
Ph balance rectifier
Anti-allergenic soap
Cockroach traps
Agar culture to test for bacteria
Anti-septic spray

Celebrated hypochondriac climber Sir Eden Janet Hadrian managed to scale the entire public lavatory suite at all 4 London railway termini, 1889.

True and False

True: *You can catch very unpleasant diseases from lavatory seats.*
You have to be a contortionist to do it.
Washing is good for you.
Soap helps.

False: *Washing is bad for you.*
Brushing your teeth makes them fall out.
Listening to the radio in the bath addles your brain.
Bidet was a French lieutenant with Napoleon.

BRAIN WORMS

Brain Worms usually live in other people's houses, gardens, and in public places. You can catch them from the lavatory, in food, off crockery, bedding, underneath their seats, carpets and the backs of settees.

Do The Worms Live In All Of Those Places?

Worms tend to inhabit all of these places but principally those belonging to people who are lower down the social scale than you are. Sometimes worms will live in the houses and gardens of people who are on the same social scale as you are, but who you do not like.

How Do They Travel?

The worm is picked up on your hand where it hooks its tail into the skin on the fingers; once there it is almost impossible to shake off, and it is so small that it is invisible to the naked eye. When you next touch your head - to scratch an ear, pick your nose or rub an eye, the Worm dislodges quickly and makes its way into your head via one of the natural orifices.

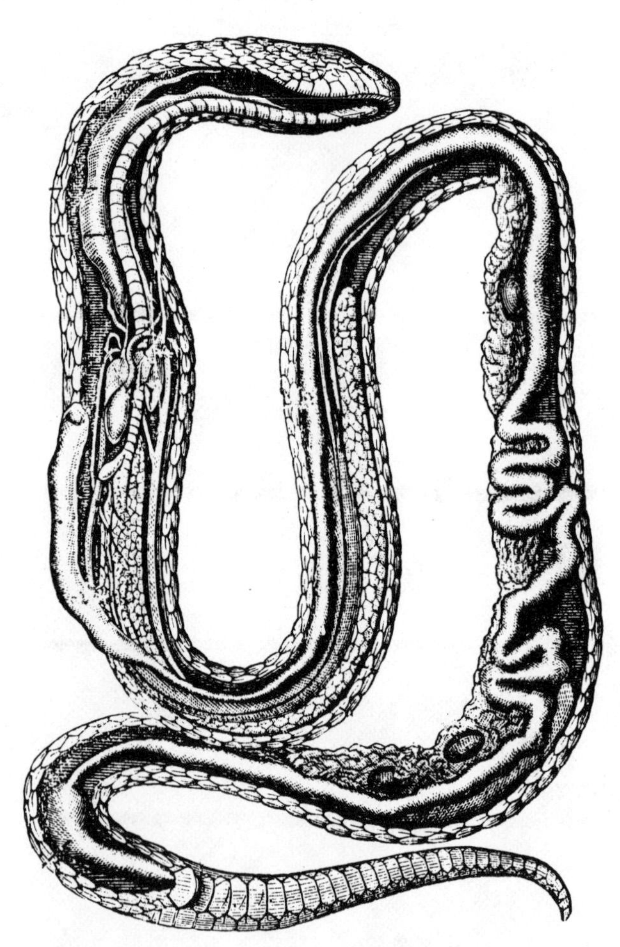

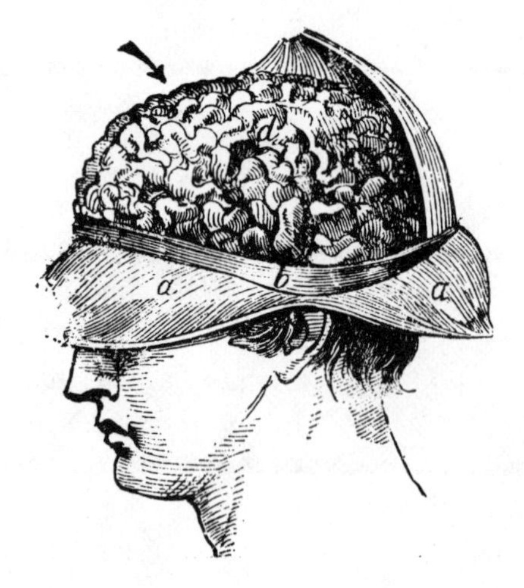

Figure 1: Brain Worms Nesting in Patient's I.Q. Area

What Do The Worms Do?

The Worms cause character defects by eating molecular portions of the relevant piece of the brain. There are no outward symptoms, the patient feels no discomfort and his or her close associates will not notice any difference and the natural life span is not impaired. However these Worms are responsible for diminishing the patient's potential in life.

I had an elderly patient who complained of never winning a Pentathlon; there seemed no good reason till I made in-depth investigations and found Brain Worms. Other of my patients complained of lack of success in merchant banking, public speaking and sexual relations; all were suffering similarly from these Worms. If you feel that people are doing unjustifiably better in life than you are, it may well be worth having yourself de-Wormed.

Figure 2: Lunching off Patient's Libido

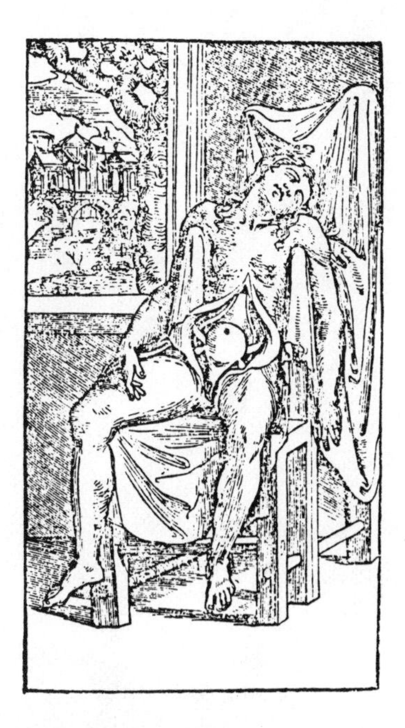

Figure 3: Destroying Patient's Energy Quotient

ROUGHAGE

Many of the problems that our parents and grandparents suffered would not have happened if they had kept to the diet of their grandparents. The simple foods of yesteryear were rich in fibre, roughage and natural goodness.

Roughage is the key to avoiding nearly every known disease and there is hardly any excuse for anyone to get ill anymore.

What is the best way to get your daily roughage?

Every person over the age of sixteen needs to consume the rather awesome figure of 12 lbs of fibrous roughage *per day*. I emphasise these figures to show just how much you really have to ingest to be good for you.

These days getting that vital roughage is no problem. A sample diet sheet below gives you an idea of how exciting roughage can be.

Breakfast
Tea, kippers, toast, gammon, poached eggs.

Lunch
Cheeseburger, chips, coke, chocolate brownie.

Supper
Liver pâté, chicken croquettes, mashed potato, wine, cheese, gâteau.

This has only ingested two ounces of fibre. Before retiring insert the remaining 11 lbs 14 oz rectally with the Karamazov Fibre Injector.

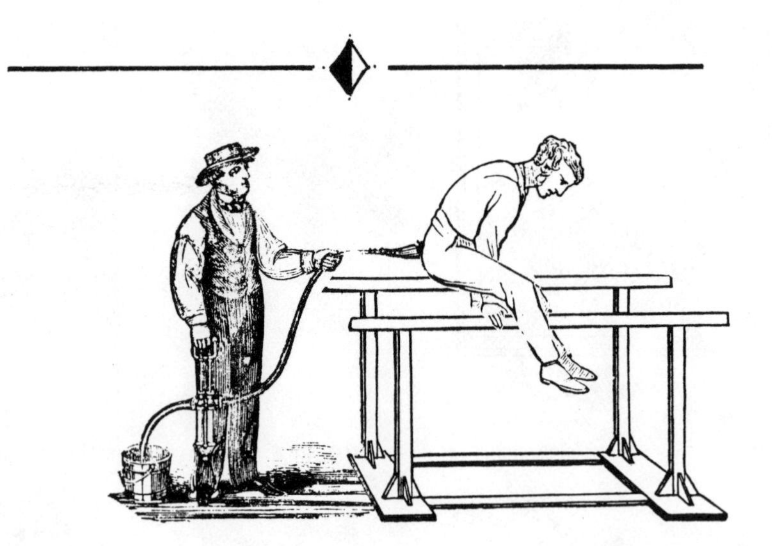

DOCTORS

Doctors are worrying. Very worrying. For people who have trained seven years they seem to take illness very lightly indeed. They are quite capable of claiming that you do not have Yellow Fever despite the fact you're suffering all the symptoms according to The Reader's Digest Book of Family Health. This is the moment when you begin to consider changing your doctor, wondering where he trained, if he trained, if he didn't just pick up a white coat and walk into the surgery. But you wish to be polite so you ask him to run some tests - he's reluctant but you make it clear that you will not leave his surgery until he does - this, along with threats to scream - usually brings positive results.

Tests: medical tests are a godsend to the Hypochondriac. Not only are there literally thousands of them, but they can take up to four weeks to process, thus allowing the Hypochondriac some really serious worrying. And of course the tests themselves can be a source of concern - ramming tubes up very small holes and wiggling them about can cause major problems. Even taking a blood sample has its hazards. Is the needle clean? Does the nurse know what to do? What if it slips and severs a nerve?

Waiting Rooms: After hospitals, waiting rooms must be the best place to pick up a rare disease. With all those sick people filing through day after day some germs must get left behind. A Hypochondriac will therefore take certain elemental precautions:

1. *Wear a surgical mask - this will filter out most common germs and also insure you get to the head of the queue - the other patients will not want to be in the same room with someone who has to wear a mask.*

2. *Wear rubber gloves - who knows what ghastly skin diseases have been smeared over the door handles.*

3. *Bring your own magazines - microbes can live in the pages of Punch for up to six months.*

THE HYPOCHONDRIAC ABROAD

All hypochondriacs instinctively know that travel abroad is a health risk. By whatever means you choose to get there you are bound to suffer. By boat you will be seasick, by plane and you will be terrified of falling out of the sky, being hijacked or going into labour.

Once abroad your real problems begin. While most unpleasant foreign diseases have now either been eradicated or can be vaccinated against, it is almost impossible to avoid using the language. All sorts of oral diseases can be caught from attempting to speak a foreign language - you have no idea who has been using the words before you or for what purpose. Just asking the way in French or ordering a pizza in Italian can infect the mouth with painful sores as well as a deep sense of inadequacy. It is much safer to stick to English - if people refuse to understand you simply repeat the phrase only louder.

Useful sign language for travel abroad

1. I am allergic to blue cheese.

2. I have Webber's Disease and need urgent medical treatment.

3. Don't breathe garlic all over me you smelly foreigner.

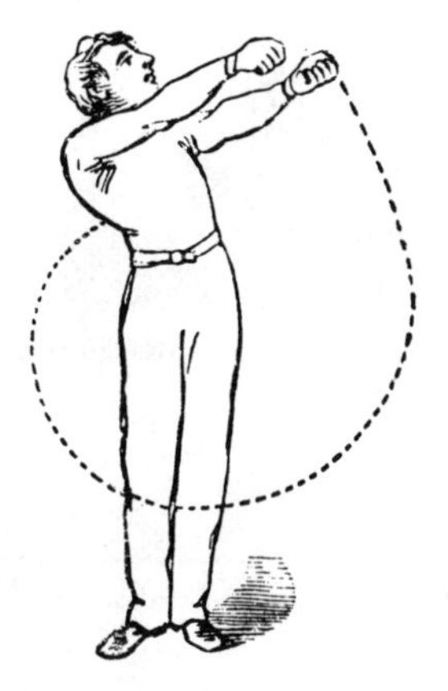

4. I am about to throw up.

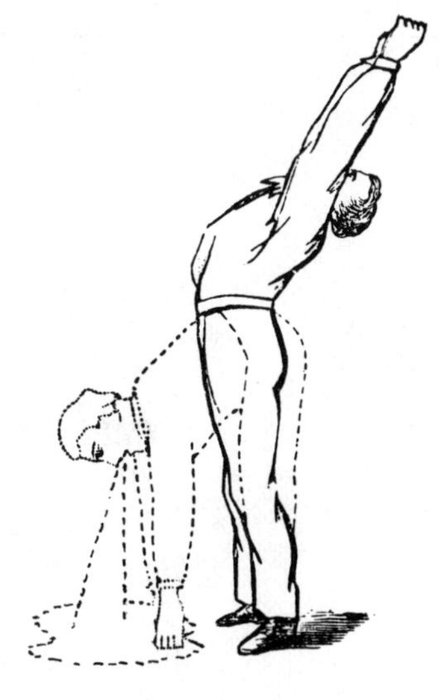

5. I'm sorry, I have just thrown up over your feet. You should learn International Sign Language.

HOW TO SLIP YOUR SYMPTOMS INTO CONVERSATION

Unfortunately you cannot always rely on people asking you how you are - especially if they have known you for some time. So some subtle ways have to be contrived to turn the conversation to your illnesses. Here are some sample opening lines:

Them:	"Nice weather we're having."
You:	"You're not hypersensitive to ultra-violet , then?"
Them:	"What's the time?"
You:	"Let me see, I've taken the green pills but haven't had the injection; it must be 4.46."
Them:	"That'll be £5.98."
You:	"That's more than my prescription for this sub-cutaneous boil."
Them:	"...or there's the Boeuf de Lapsidine..."
You:	"Was it fed on organic food? My stomach ulcer's very sensitive."
Them:	"You don't look very well ..."
You:	"I don't like to talk about it ..."

THE WRONG DIAGNOSIS

SYMPTOM: *Yellow Eyes and Diarrhoea*

FIRST DIAGNOSIS: *Possibly an attack of Liverishness or mild Jaundice.*

REAL PROBLEM: Rabies; it is possible to catch rabies from things other than animals, including insects and even inanimate objects; in this case it may have been caught from a lavatory seat.

HANGOVERS

A hangover is the body's way of telling you that something is wrong - usually that you have had six gins too many. The throbbing head, aching limbs and strong desire to die are simply Nature telling you to back off. However, Nature does not always know best - if you hadn't had those six gins you might never have dared ask Deirdre out – on the other hand Deirdre might have laughed a lot less if you'd stuck to orange juice.

Fortunately there is relief from hangovers. Since the pains are caused by excess alcohol on the brain all that is necessary is to remove this liquid as painlessly as possible. To this end simply drill a hole in the skull and drain off anything that smells of alcohol. When the liquid begins to turn red and more viscous you may experience a sensation of dizziness - this is the moment to stop.

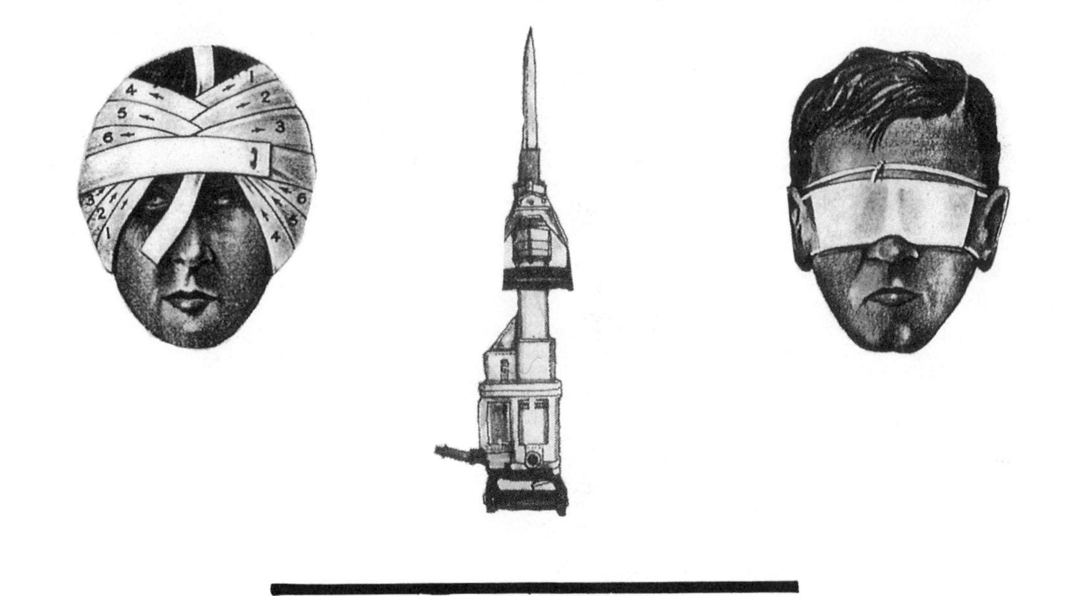

THE WRONG DIAGNOSIS

SYMPTOM: *Severe Headaches*

FIRST DIAGNOSIS: *Migraine*

REAL PROBLEM: An abnormally brutal haircut several years ago may have tugged at the roots of the hair and loosened small parts of the brain at the same time; this may cause character changes.

PHONEAMIA

Description: This allergy started in the United States and has spread worldwide in just a few decades. From a rather quaint and rare disorder, often laughed at, it has now become an epidemic affecting over a third of the world's population and is spreading rapidly. Highly contagious, it is enough to know someone with a phone - the desire to own one's own soon follows, and from that point on the disease takes hold.

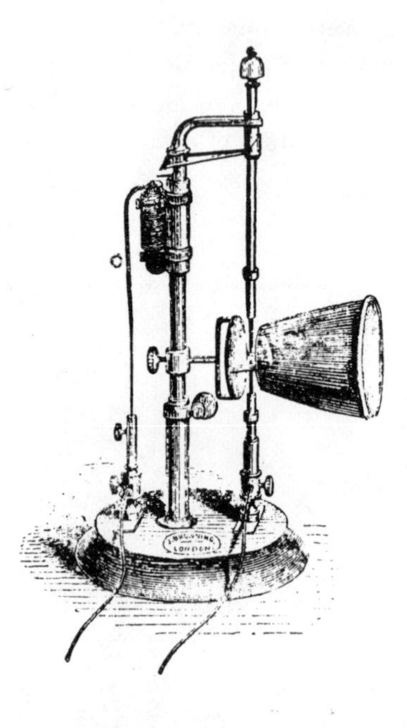

Symptoms: The major symptom is to pick up a phone, usually during peak hours, and make totally unnecessary forty-minute long-distance calls. The disease then lies dormant for up to three months, when it suddenly manifests itself in the form of a very large bill and threats to remove your line if payment is not received within seven (7) days.

An equally dangerous strain, Phonitis Teenagium, attacks parents with children who insist on conducting their entire social life over the telephone. This leads to pathological repetition of certain phrases, such as 'Get off that phone' or 'Have you any idea how much that is costing me?' followed by threats to install a pay-phone.

Treatment: Surgical removal of both phone and line is the only complete answer. However, the effects of the disease can be lessened by strict use of a stopwatch or, failing this, a nagging partner or housemate. Withdrawal symptoms can be severe, including unashamed use of other people's phones and attempts to push foreign coins into pay-phones.

BEING BURIED ALIVE

1 in 13,000 people get buried alive. Although of relatively short duration being buried alive can be extremely unpleasant – the victim often wears his nails and skin to the bone in a futile attempt to scrape a way out.

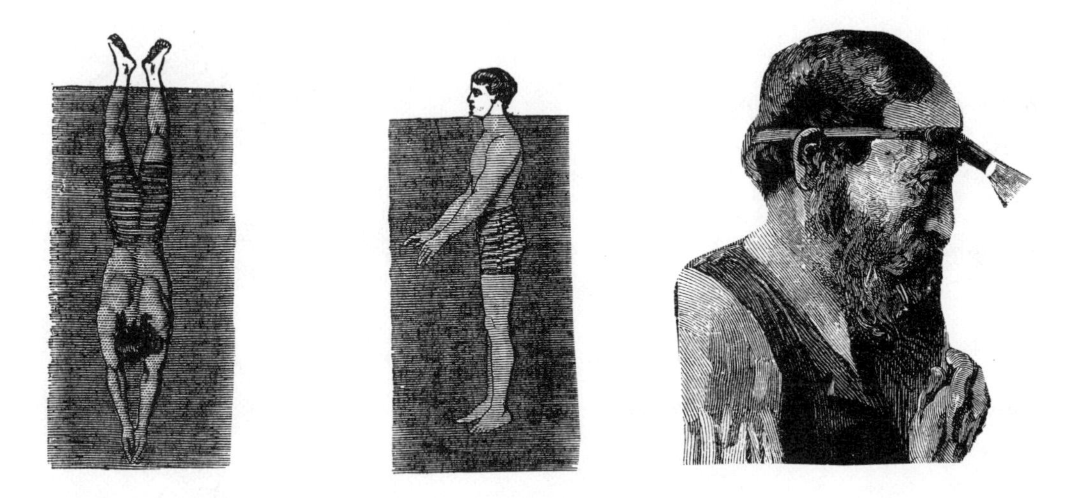

However, some very simple precautions can guarantee this will not happen.

1. Ascertain that you are truly dead. If you still enjoy the Radio Times this could mean you are dead but might mean you are just a cabbage. Check by dipping into The Spectator – if you agree with more than two articles you are either dead or should be. If you are still alive:

2. Pack an emergency Life Kit in your coffin. Suggested items include: thermos flask of coffee (you don't want to fall asleep); a book to while away the hours; a drill to make an air vent; a whistle to attract attention; a torch to read the book with; a pen and paper to write to your doctor complaining of mis-diagnosis.

THE MEANING OF LIFE

Fortunately this need no longer be a worry since I discovered the meaning of life back in 1976 during the course of my researches. See my article 'Life: Meaning and Worry' in the Lancet, Vol 34, 1977.

PLACEBOS

Sometimes in an attempt to divert you from the gravity of your illness doctors prescribe fake remedies, often known as placebos. If you're worried, watch out for unusual shapes, strange lettering or a slightly sweet taste.

Often prescribed for recurring foot pains.

Not for appendicitis.

Commonly claimed to be an anti-biotic.

Fake treatment for gangrene.

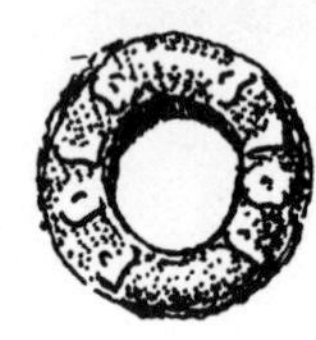

ACCIDENT BLACK SPOTS

(and how to avoid them)

Headrests in buses, trains, planes etc.

More than just dandruff can be caught from headrests. This is because many carriers of infection may well be suffering brain damage and could sit in the seat the wrong way round and breathe germs into the headrest. The only safe answer is either to stand, which of course is difficult in aeroplanes, to place a lead shield between the headrest and your head or to sit on the headrest itself (which is also difficult in aeroplanes).

Ballpoint pens

Remember that some disgusting people do not just stick their ballpoint pens in their mouths but in all their other body orifices. Never use other people's pens.

WATER

Many Hypochondriacs seem to think that mineral water is not good for you. But just consider this – as the so-called pure water cascades through the Alps what else is it picking up along with minerals and vital salts? All sorts of nasty microbes from the dead sheep further up-stream, not to mention the chemical plant that discharges directly into the same water table, or the acid rain that falls all over the area.

It is far preferable to collect your own water which you can then boil, filter and purify.

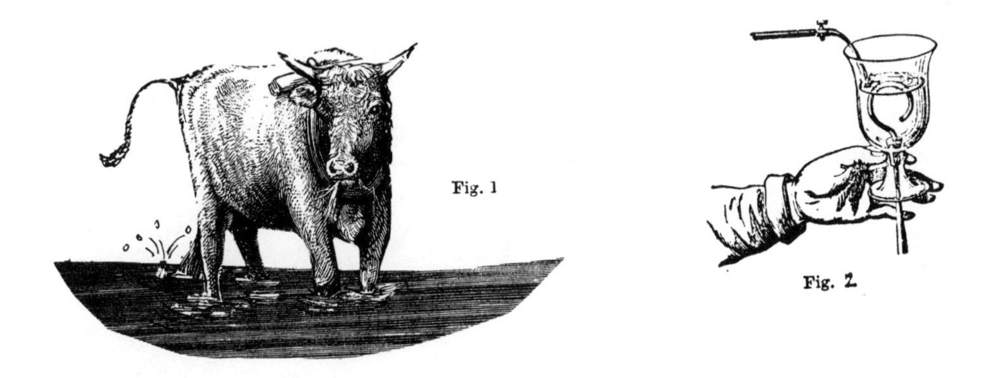
Fig. 1

Fig. 2

TELL-TALE SIGNS TO LOOK OUT FOR

We all feel tired, below par and washed out from time to time. But do you sometimes feel like that for no reason at all?

The natural state of the body is to feel keen, vigorous, alert and full of energy all the time. If you do not then there is clearly a reason.

Try this little test: Spend a typical day at the office or doing the housework at home; eat a hurried meal and do some more work; put the kids to bed; do some more work; take six hours sleep yourself; repeat for ten years. You should feel like a million dollars, if not you should examine your life style.

I Asked My Doctor But He Told Me Not To Worry

Many doctors overlook these tell-tale signs. Only you can tell if there is something to really worry about.

Sometimes I Don't Feel Tired, Irritable and Listless, At All

Then there is nothing to worry about is there?

But Then Sometimes I Do

Well then there is, isn't there?

CHECKING OUT YOUR PARTNER

When you sleep with someone for the first time it is as well to remember that you are not sleeping with them but with their diseases, previous partners and their previous partners' diseases. Therefore it is essential to know as much as possible about your lover's past. This is a delicate and sensitive area and must be approached subtly without giving offence.

Bring up the subject of previous lovers in a playful, lighthearted manner, slipping them a copy of the chart below to fill in:

Ex-Lover's Name	Address
Date of birth	
NHS Number	
Sexual Contacts over last 3 years	Unusual marks

If during early fumblings you come across a vaccination mark this is a good opportunity to bring up the subject of countries visited, precautions taken and possibly to ask for a look at medical certificates.

As further progress is made you can disguise more detailed examination as foreplay.Run your fingers through their hair murmuring how soft and silky it is at the same time checking for lice, fleas and head worms. Gentle stroking of the main body areas will identify any boils, sores and rashes.

Introduce a thermometer as a sex toy and explain how sensuous giving a blood sample can be. You can then go on to claim that gargling with antiseptic is an ancient Indian aphrodisiac and should precede all kissing.

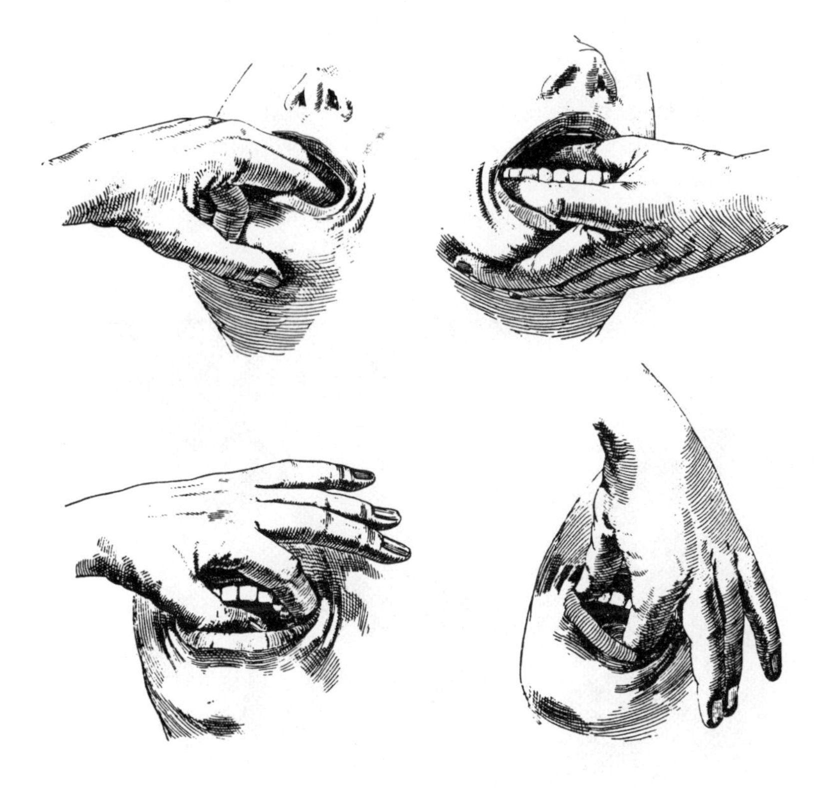

KISSING

This is about the most unhygienic thing that can happen to you and it is obvious that it should be avoided if possible at any cost. It is feasible that however hard you have tried that you may end up in a 'kissing' situation. In that unhappy case you should, having personally inspected the other party's medical record, follow the procedure below.

1. Gargle with an industrial strength mouth wash – this is often sold under brand-names such as 'Liquid-Plumber' or 'Strip-it'.

2. Spray your partner's mouth with one of the above, being sure to brush cheek, jowls, gums and teeth with steel wool.

3. Place condom over tongue.

4. Inflate balloon in partner's mouth.

5. Carefully insert your tongue (in condom) into balloon opening.

Violent wiggling may break the balloon. It is advised that kissing does not continue for more than thirty seconds at a time, since after this both parties usually feel like throwing up. A safer alternative is to kiss by mail only.

SEX

Sex is very probably the most worrying thing you can do. A thousand things can go wrong. It is so worrying that one might well choose to do without it altogether if it weren't for the fact that not having sex is even more worrying than having it. Most people are worried about their sexual performance. Worrying about worrying about one's sexual performance can also impede it. This is disturbing. Here are just a few of the things that can go wrong:

P.E. or Premature Ejaculation

This worry related condition is extremely embarrassing and humiliating especially as it can happen at any time. Chronic sufferers have been known to experience premature ejaculation anything up to three years before the date of actual sexual contact. This is difficult for even the most sympathetic of partners to understand.

If you suffer from P.E. try explaining to your partner that it *was* a wonderful experience, the earth *did* move, only it happened three months before on the 37 bus from Peckham.

While it may not always be possible to achieve simultaneous orgasm, with time and practice you should be able to narrow it down to within the same week. To do this simply worry about something else. With the psyche working overtime trying to solve the Third World debt, the penis will manage very well on its own. Just tape a list of worries to your pillow and concentrate on them at the height of passion. Here is a brief list of possible Pillow Panics:

What if they hear next door?
Does yoghurt go off after ten days?
What did Billy Holiday die of?
Am I a thought in someone else's mind? (only for serious cases)
Will it rain tomorrow?

Foreplay

Foreplay is of course of vital importance. It is no good simply rushing into the sexual act with no time to consider the awful consequences. The practised worrier can extend this period into a prolonged act in itself, indeed the mature couple may be able to render actual sex completely unnecessary . . .

"Will she mind if I touch her breast?"
"What if he touches my breast – what shall I do?"
"If she doesn't like it what shall I say?"
"If he does and I say nothing will he think I'm easy?"
"If I don't will she think I'm not interested?"
"If he does and I say something will he think I'm frigid?"
"If I do and she says something will she mean it or will she just be saying it?"
"If I say nothing but kiss him will he think I'm too quick?"
"If I do and then kiss her will she think that's all I'm interested in? Is that all I'm interested in?"
"If he thinks I'm too quick will he lose respect for me? If he doesn't respect me can he love me? Could I love someone who didn't respect me?"
"Can one be interested in someone solely on a sexual level? Is it possible to be interested in anybody except on a sexual level? To what level does the sexual level go? What does the idea of a level imply?"

Orgasms

Orgasms are, of course, the big one when it comes to sex worries. Am I getting enough? Am I giving enough? Are they shattering enough? Do they exist? Would I recognise one if I met it at a party? How do you have small talk with an orgasm? Does anybody else get them standing in an open-top bus reading a soup tin?

I am often asked if orgasms shorten life. This, of course, is an old wives tale with no truth in it - however, it can be some comfort if you are not getting any orgasms at all.

Pregnancy

Women are more likely to get pregnant than men. But this should not stop men worrying about pregnancy altogether, for although women alone have been producing babies for the last 10,000 years, we are about due for an evolution change and YOU might be the first! As for women, pregnancy offers almost the perfect subject for worry - by alternately worrying that you *ARE* pregnant and that you're *NOT*, it can prove a source of anxiety for most of your life. When it ceases to be a problem it is a simple matter to transfer the worry to fear of being past it, and generally useless.

Men

Women find men very worrying. They worry that men don't like them, they worry that men do like them. They worry that men are bastards, and that they're not.

Women

Men worry that they are women. This is quite normal. Sometimes I think that I'm a pomegranate.

SAFE SEX

Coming into contact with another human being is at best hazardous but to voluntarily exchange body fluids is hypochondriacal suicide. However, it is now possible to have 'safe sex'. This simply means not touching your partner. Safe sex can take place over the phone, through the mail or, in extreme cases, via a mutual friend.

If you find yourself in a situation where there is no time to run the above checks, and where it would be ungracious not to sleep with someone (an Embassy party for example), be sure to wear the specially designed Karamazov Protective Suit.

DR KARAMAZOV'S SURGERY

Symptoms:	*Wet ear.*
Diagnosis:	*Someone has their tongue in your ear.*
Treatment:	*Remove with pair of gardening shears.*
Symptoms:	*No feeling in the head or upper neck.*
Diagnosis:	*You have been guillotined.*
Treatment:	*See a specialist.*
Symptoms:	*Wake up barking in the middle of the night; urinate against walls.*
Diagnosis:	*You are turning into a dog.*
Treatment:	*Get yourself put down.*

Premature Evolution

Around your twentieth birthday, and again about the time of your thirtieth, you may start to notice some of the other tell-tale signs of premature evolution. These are:-

1) *Receding hairline*
2) *Lower tolerance to alcohol*
3) *Joints becoming slightly less supple*
4) *Inability to do it twice a night*
5) *Wanting to go to bed before 2 a.m.*
6) *One or two grey pubic hairs*

With Premature Evolution the victims telescope generations, and perform the evolution of centuries in a few years becoming very clever and wise but at the same time taking on the appearance of humans as they will become in the year 2995 - that is balding, probably plump, short-sighted, interested in gardening, TV and going to bed early.

THE WRONG DIAGNOSIS

SYMPTOM: *Sneezing*

FIRST DIAGNOSIS: *Onset of a cold; hay fever.*

REAL PROBLEM: Wind; a gross excess of flatulence-producing food (baked beans) had been consumed and the sneezing was a type of extra emergency *safety valve* operating.

The Little Toe

Many people have written to me in the past asking just what is happening to their little toes?

Perhaps you have not examined your little toe enough to notice that it is very much smaller than the others, is bent and appears to have no bone in it; also that its nail needs cutting far less frequently than the others. Why?

The answer is that for a long time now the Russians have been developing a number of Biological warfare weapons in their research establishment at Portonski, just inside the East German border. In 1961 and again in 1978 there was a considerable escape of chemicals due to bottle caps not being screwed on properly, and the prevailing westerly winds blew these chemicals over Europe and the USA.

For a while Western monitoring units noticed nothing, but it now seems that the chemical was in fact *235 meta* Darwin, a synthetic gene-attacking peptide that hastens evolution. The disappearance of our little toe is one of the signs of Premature Evolution, a worrying phenomenon that seemed to be occurring by itself (perhaps because of background radioactivity) before the escape of this chemical alarmed scientists the world over.

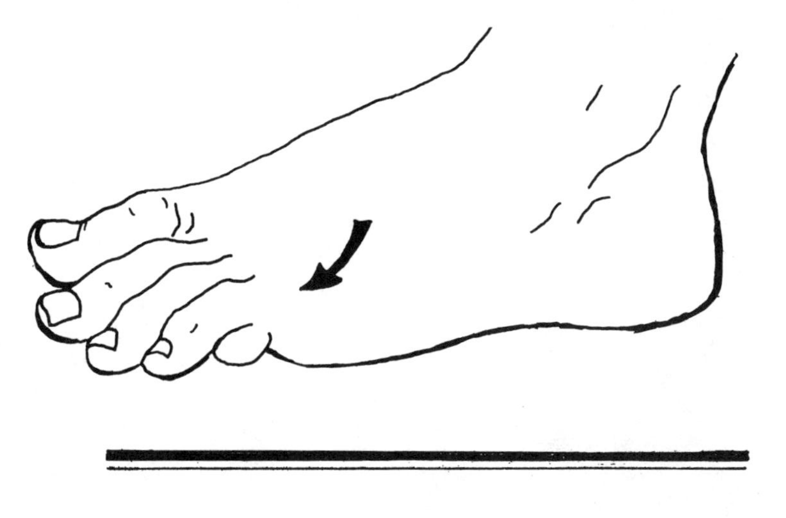

HAIR

To remove or not to remove. In this ecologically aware age it may be thought barbarous to remove natural undergrowth and replace it with eau de cologne. However, there is also the worry of what thinks of your undergrowth as home – all sorts of nasty little creatures, most of them intent on sucking your blood. You've only got eight pints so one can't be too careful. One too many nosebleeds and it'd have to be hospital and a thoroughly unpleasant transfusion, and who knows whose blood they're pumping into your veins, with what bugs and diseases. It is therefore safer to remove all trace of hair from your entire body.

DRAWING ATTENTION

One of the most difficult tasks facing the Hypochondriac is getting the right sort of attention. The first incidence of heart failure will have the family panicking, the emergency services working flat out and you strapped into the Intensive Care Unit within minutes. However, on the twelfth occurrence, when once again it turns out to be a bad case of wind, sympathy begins to run out. This only serves to worry the Hypochondriac further, perhaps inducing heart failure - what if it was the real thing and nobody took any notice? To avoid this possibility it is best to be prepared with a series of attention-gathering strategies should the thirteenth and real emergency occur. These are listed in order of severity and should not be used out of sequence.

1. **Shout**
2. **Scream**
3. **Wave arms**
4. **Go very, very quiet**
5. **Dribble**
6. **Throw-up**
7. **Babble**
8. **Babble while throwing-up**
9. **Roll eyes**
10. **Lunge at someone**
11. **Lunge at someone and throw-up over them, and roll eyes**
12. **Offer money**

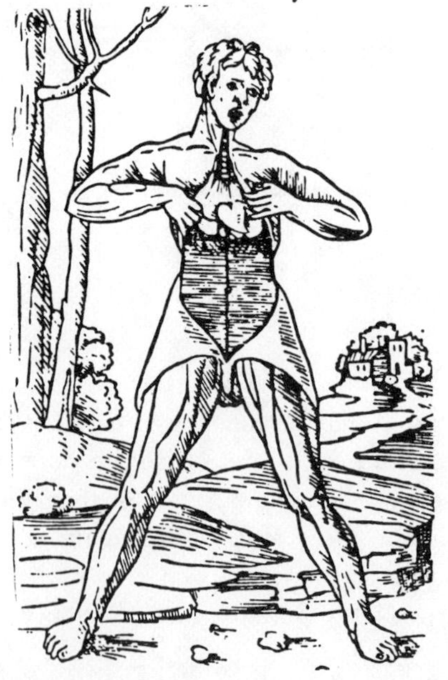

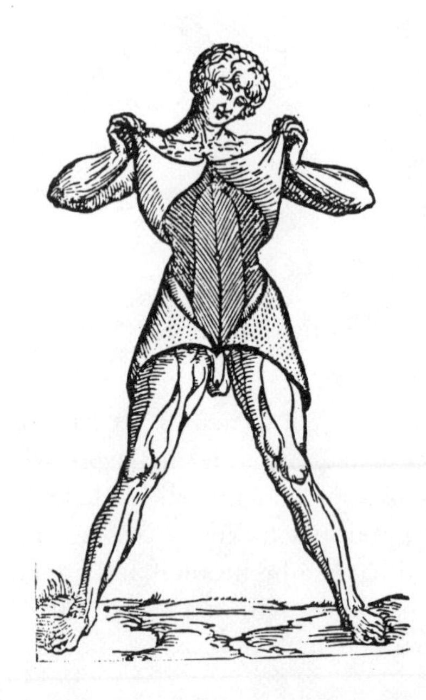

SWEAT

We all sweat – all that is except the people in deodorant commercials. Perspiration is nothing to be ashamed about – it is simply nature's way of cooling us off – admittedly it might have been neater to install air-conditioning but we must put up with what we have.

Excess sweating, however, can be very dangerous. If, for some reason, the body thinks you need cooling down when you don't it can soon drain you of all vital body fluids, not to mention losing you several intimate friends.

If you are sweating profusely this could be for a number of reasons:

1. You are hot – go somewhere cool.

2. You are about to be shot – this is no time to worry about sweating, try remembering the Lord's prayer.

3. You are running – stop. All hypochondriacs know that any unnecessary movement can be a health risk.

4. You are in bed with someone you love – use the sheets to dab discreetly – if you love someone why sweat all over them?

CONSTIPATION

Constipation is an embarrassing condition – people do not like to talk about it and frankly I do not even like to write about it.

KARAMAZOV INK TESTS

Psychological health is of as great if not more importance than physiological health. To this end I have devised a simple psychological test to enable anyone to have instant insight into their subconscious. Based on years of clinical experience and a particularly fruitful bath one Wednesday afternoon the Karamazov Ink Test is an infallible guide to Man's Inner Being and a pretty good indication of his waist size too.

Place the Tests under a good, though not dazzling, light and allow your eyes to wander over them. After a few minutes the blots will seem to take on new shapes and forms, arranging themselves into clear pictures and images. When this happens simply write down what you see. After you have finished all six you can analyse the results.

Figure 1 - *Is generally thought by most normal people to look like a mouse playing the piano.*

Figure 2 - *Should look like your mother.*

Figure 3 - Was labelled a 'chocolate motor car' by 98% of interviewees in a Chicago poll taken in 1958.

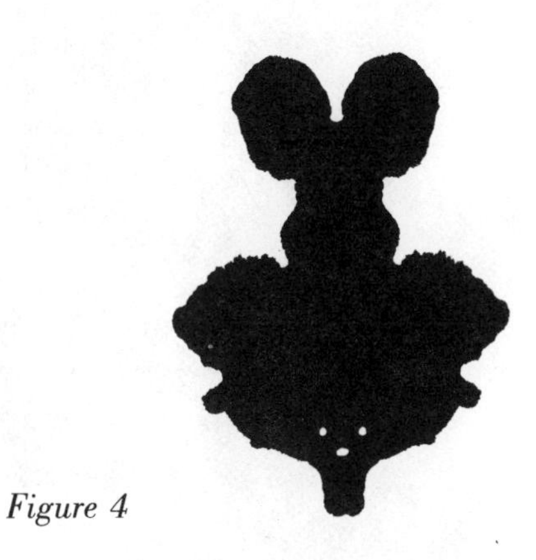

Figure 4

- Should look like a Viking helmet.

Figure 5 - Should resemble an axe murderer.

Figure 6 - Should look like an ink blot unless you are suffering from Rorschach's Disease.

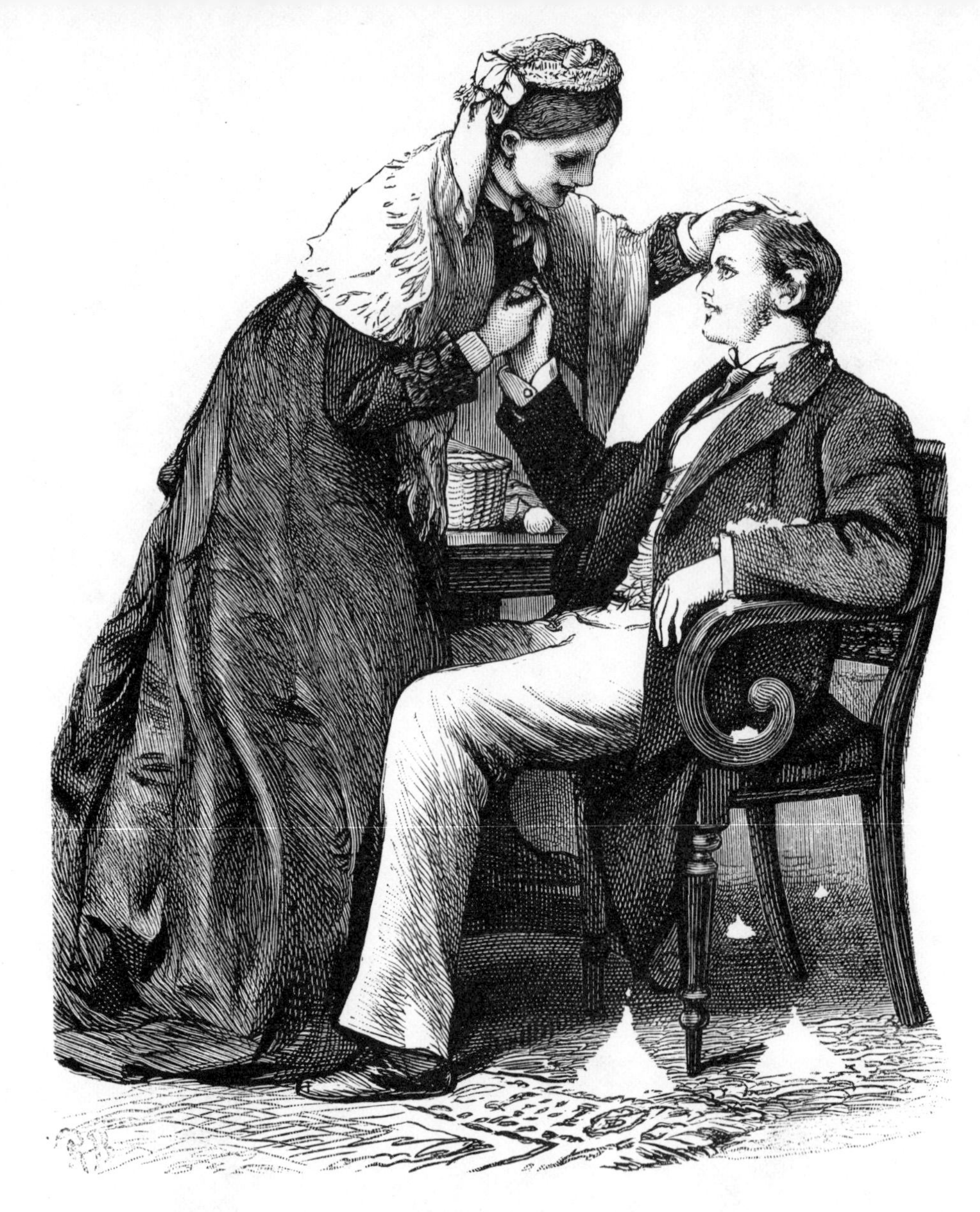

DANDRUFF

Many people think dandruff is simply an embarrassing but minor complaint. This is typical of the complacency of non-worriers. My extensive researches into this disease have conclusively shown that chronic dandruff impairs mental efficiency and can bring on psychosis. This is really quite obvious when you consider where the little white bits come from - the scalp - and what does the scalp contain? - the brain. In a nutshell dandruff is the gradual shedding of the brain itself. This explains why sufferers always look a little down-in-the-mouth and do not notice that their shoulders are covered in a fine snow of dead tissue - their perceptive faculties are literally being worn away. Fortunately, there is a cure - not a very pleasant one but effectiveness is what we are looking for here. The patient simply dunks his head every morning into a vat of pig's fat. This adheres to the scalp and prevents any more tissue breaking away. Side effects include throwing up and a life of celibacy.

The 'Nouvel' Diseases

These late twentieth century dietary diseases are generally called *Nouvel* because they were discovered in France, in the 1970's by a Frenchman, Prof. Petitbouffe, working at the Hôpital de l'Estomac Sacré in Lyon.

The symptoms are easily confused with other complaints, such as hunger and even starvation, but an accurate diagnosis can be made by answering the questions below:

a) Do you suffer from between meal hunger?

b) Do you suffer from post meal hunger?

c) At the end of a meal do you feel like you need a Mars bar?

d) Are you losing weight?

e) Are you losing money?

f) Does the sight of raspberry purée and dandelion leaves make you ill?

If you answer Yes to any of the above then you may well be sickening for one of the Nouvel diseases; however, as with other 'social' diseases a change in your habits may prevent further infection or the catching of the illness in the first place. A determined attack at the first symptom can knock it on the head:

SYMPTOM	TREATMENT
A Mousseline of three vegetables with a whisky, crab and chocolate sauce.	A Big Mac
Crispy packets of crayfish and armadillo farci avec Anis; sauce Espadrille.	Cod and chips, twice
Roulade des langues d'escargots, stir fried with daffodils, aspic and prunes.	Jelly and custard
Tiny fritters of fresh dill seeds cooked in their own juice on a bed of steamed lemon pips, the whole garnished with a petit pois.	Salt & Vinegar Crisps

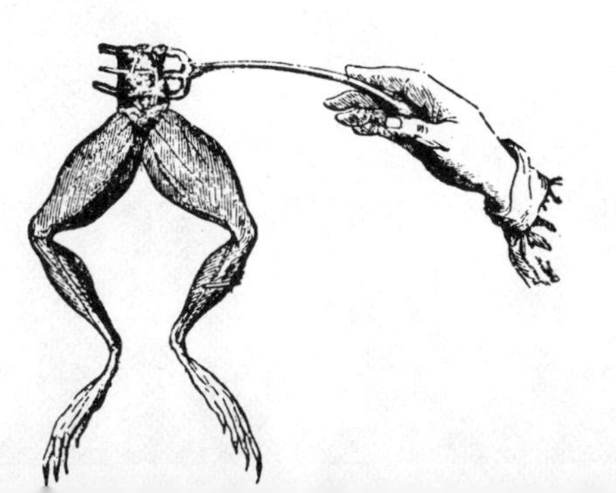

KILOBYTE

Description: This increasingly popular disease is largely mental, consisting of a strong belief that computers save time, effort and money. Once Kilobyte has taken hold it is very difficult to shake - despite all evidence to the contrary the patient continues to put faith in technology. A typical case history would consist of the victim being lured into purchasing the machine by either an old friend, colleague or brash young salesman.

Symptoms: The disease then goes through several phases:

1. **Manualitis** - a series of very late nights as the patient struggles to understand the manual, and work out where the on/off switch is. Can take up to three weeks. Symptoms include red eyes, sore fingers and a tendency to throw the manual against the VDU.

2. **Floppies** - this is perhaps the only enjoyable phase of the disease - having mastered the basics the patient feels that he completely understands not only his machine but the whole computer revolution. In a fit of enthusiasm he enters all his records onto floppy discs and throws away the originals.

3. **Wipeum Syndrome** - the final stage of the disease when the computer, apparently on a whim of its own, decides to wipe out all the information you have just stored. Symptoms include incredulous staring at the screen, rattling of floppy discs followed rapidly by unconsciousness and unemployment.

Treatment: Once the disease has run its full course most patients have no desire to mix with any technology ever again and revert to sucking pencils.

HOSPITALS

More people die in hospitals than anywhere else. This is sobering enough in itself, but coupled with the fact that more diseases are spread through hospitals than anywhere else it is sufficient argument to avoid these places like the plague, which after all, they in many ways resemble.

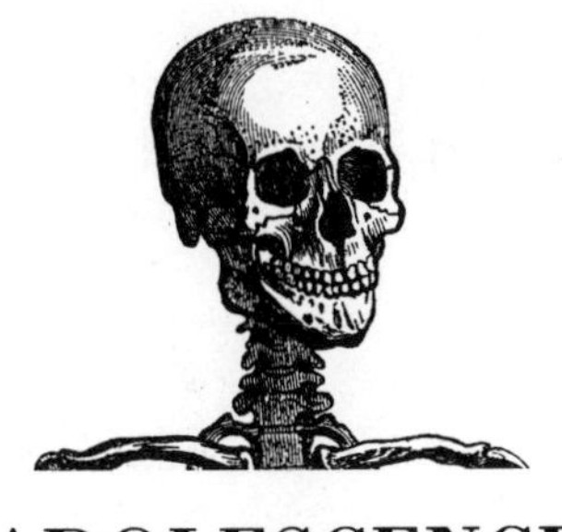

ADOLESCENCE

Adolescence is a complaint that most people suffer until their late thirties. It consists mostly of the mistaken belief that one will suddenly fall in love with someone who is madly in love with you and you will both live happily ever after; this and becoming Famous. The only cure for adolescence is bitterness.

TELL-TALE SIGNS OF AWFUL THINGS

Early Morning Stiffness is another of those little symptoms, apparently quite benign, that can sometimes have a very different meaning.

It Goes Away During The Day
If it does all well and good; but are you sure? Are there even tiny traces of it still around at lunch time?

I Don't Think So Doc
Let's hope not because of all the tell-tale signs that there are to watch out for, a severe case of Early Morning Stiffness is the most serious. It is always fatal.

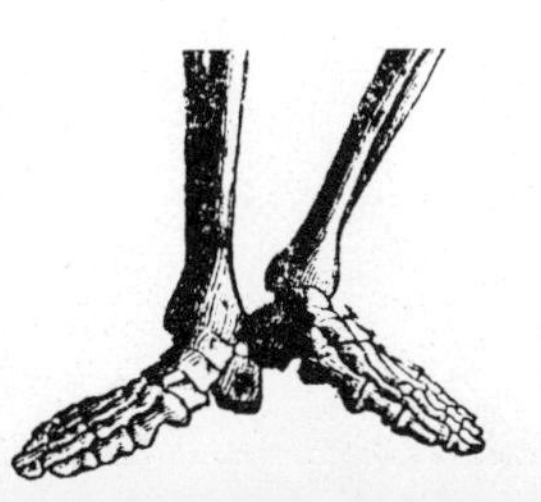

QUESTIONNAIRE

YES NO

Have You Got Questionnaire's Disease?

When You Wake Up In The Morning, Do You ....
a) Eagerly jump out of bed shouting Aieeeeeee
b) Start going back to sleep again
c) Tick off imaginary boxes with your toes

Have You Recently Looked At ....
i) Your nose
ii) Your tongue
iii) Your income tax return

Is The ....
a) World full of dog biscuits
c) Moon made of sodium glutamate
b) Meaning of life worth explaining

Do You Ever Feel ....
a) Tired
b) Tired and depressed
c) Tired, irritable and depressed
d) Like filling in a form

YES NO

Have You Noticed That ....

a) People who ask you questions in the street are getting younger
b) There are not as many bats around as there were
c) Thirty is a dangerous age

Has Your Best Friend Told You ....

c) That you are very boring
b) That he is not your best friend
c) To fill in, sign, date and return the form to him

Do You Ever Feel Worried That ....

a) Life is passing you by
b) You may not notice that a Questionnaire is misnumbered
ii) You should have been born 200 years ago

When You Lie On Your Back, Do You Feel ....

a) Sexy
h) Sleepy
i) Like answering questions

FEMININE ITCHING

Dear Doctor Karamazov,

I have a problem that I am so embarrassed about that I cannot bring myself to discuss it with my husband or even my doctor, so in despair I am writing to you, but please do not publish my name and address. My problem is that of feminine itching; I have tried all the usual treatments like changing washing powders and using creams from the chemist, all to no avail. It has been going on for about a year now but seems to get worse when I worry; the trouble is of course that I worry about it and so it gets worse; also I then worry that someone will discover my problem and it gets even worse.

Yours sincerely,

Worried, London

Mrs J. Robertson,
54 Rose Drive,
London EC4 5SW

Dear Mrs. Robertson,
Thank you for your most interesting letter. Feminine itching can indeed be a most tiresome problem and I see that you have tried to have a go at treating it by yourself. But sometimes it really is necessary to seek professional help - as in this case.

For feminine itching, whether on the back, in the hair or on the soles of the feet, I always recommend a jolly good scratch. I also advise my male patients to do the same if they have any masculine itchings.

Yours,

The Doctor

ACCIDENT BLACK SPOTS

(and how to avoid them)

Cracked Tea Cups

Salmonella, venereal diseases, whooping cough, piles - the list of germs that live in cracked crockery is horrifying. What do you do then when visiting for tea and suddenly notice that you have been given a deadly chalice?

Drinking from the other side of the cup does not, unfortunately, work - since both whooping cough and salmonella germs can swim. The only way out is to make sipping noises through clenched teeth and pour the contents of the cup over the carpet while the host is not watching.

Shaking Hands

Probably the single most dangerous action that you can perform in the course of the day, shaking hands is one of those ancient customs that our descendants will find unbelievable - a bit like brushing teeth in a toilet.

Do anything to get out of this - a friendly slap on the back, a fake bandage on the hand, keeping the hands firmly in the pocket, all are ruses that sometimes work. If they do not, making no new social contacts is the only solution. Do not visit France.

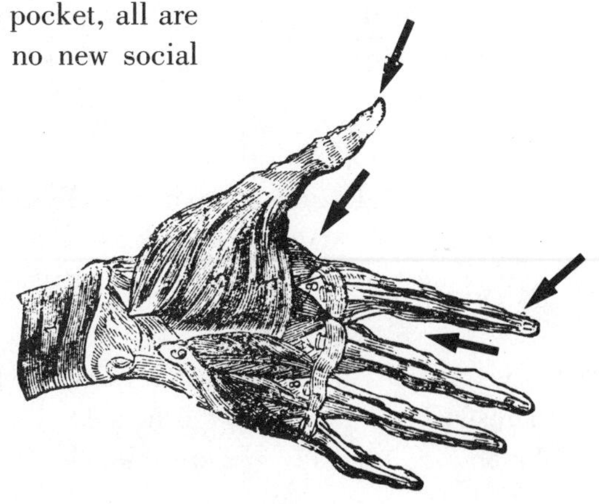

HOW TO READ MEDICINE LABELS

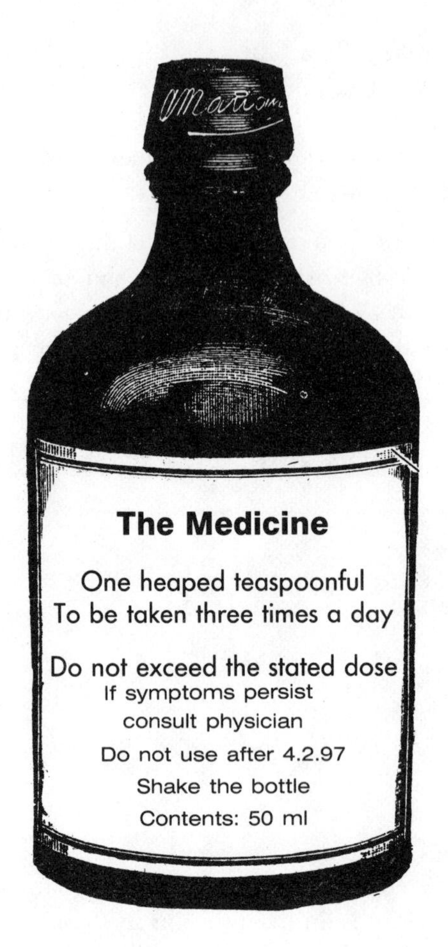

Nothing very much to worry about that you might say. Or is there? Plenty of people have been poisoned by taking the wrong medicine, so it is a wise person that takes the time to know the labels on bottles.

Let's start at the top. 'The Medicine'; the definite article 'the' gives an air of authority, but since the label is a standard printed one, how do YOU know this is YOUR medicine? The answer is of course that you do not. You do not even know if it is A medicine. Perhaps it WAS the medicine, but is it still? It could have been filled with A Poison, by a pharmacist who wanted to play THE practical joke.

'One heaped teaspoonful' sounds simple, but have you ever seen the size of teaspoons in Afghanistan? And how heaped is heaped? If 50% more or less makes no difference is the drug worth taking anyway? Already you are thinking of changing your doctor and we are only five words in.

'To be taken three times a day' . . . but when, by whom and how? Well I suppose we can assume that it is Us What Is Going To Take it, and I suppose we can assume that the three times a day means during daylight hours . . . no wait, we can assume no such thing with daylight saving time and so on. More importantly, how do we take this medicine, if such it be? Teaspoons would suggest by mouth but there is nothing to say that you do not pour it in your ear or even up your bottom.

With such poor instructions so far you would be in no mood whatsoever to 'exceed the stated dose' for fear of your life.

'Do not use . . .' blah, blah, blah – can you trust anything with a shelf life this long? The only safe procedure is to return to your doctor immediately and request he makes up a medicine tailor-made to your complaint.

THE WRONG DIAGNOSIS

SYMPTOM: *Hairy Nostrils*

FIRST DIAGNOSIS: *Nothing to worry about; hair length increases in nose and ears with age.*

REAL PROBLEM: A long hair from the nostril may in fact be a Nerve ending; when *'you suffer from Nerves'* this is what people mean; the nerves grow longer and in extreme cases protrude from the body.

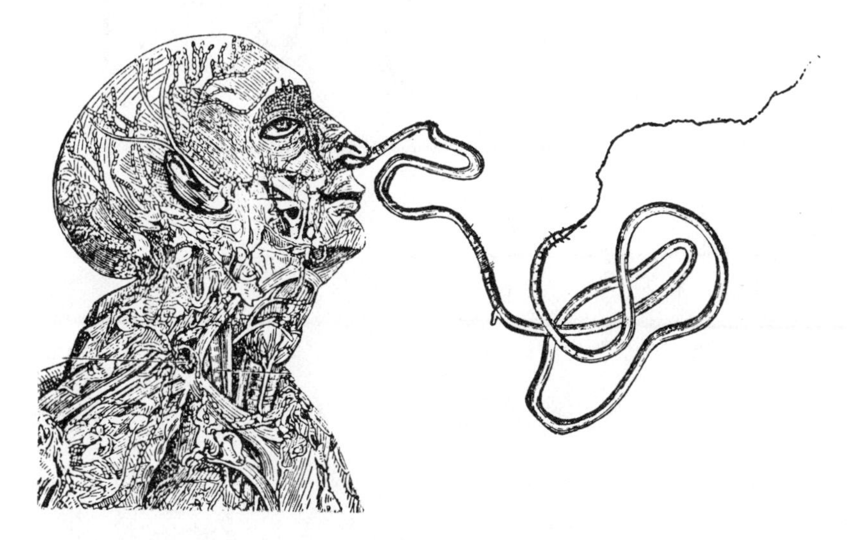

GOING TO THE SHOPS

A trip to the shops can be a hazardous business - it is as well to prepare for any eventualities that may crop up by taking along Dr Karamazov's handy First Aid Kit:

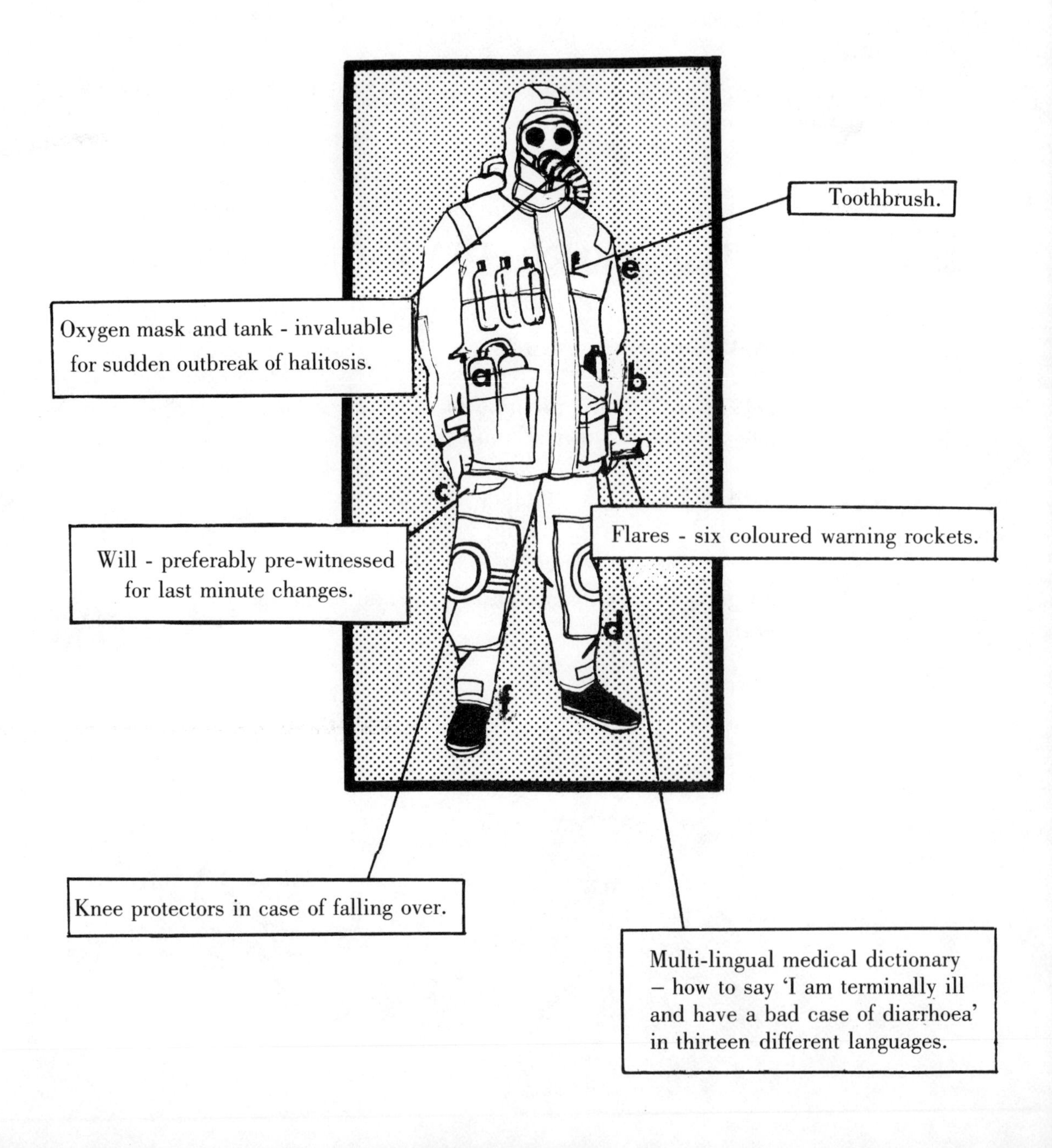

Tin of whitewash to reflect nuclear flash.

a Automatic lung – you may need this once you have lifted the 30 ton lorry from your chest. If not it still makes a handy place to store sandwiches.

b 8 pints of blood - this should be your own.

c Winch and lifting tackle - can lift up to three cars or a large lorry.

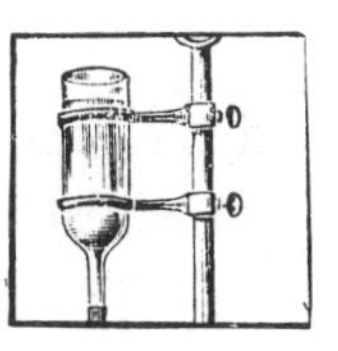

d Saline drip.

e Space blanket - this not only keeps you warm and dry but also reflects radar.

Complete Korean homeopathic medicine chest.

f Seismograph - detects coughs and sneezes up to five miles away.

ACCIDENT BLACK SPOTS

(and how to avoid them)

Hotel Bedroom Floors

It is well known that over 80% of hotel guests have serious foot diseases whose microbes can permeate socks and stockings.

Leave your shoes on at all times before retiring and then kick them off, without touching the floor while sitting on the bed. If you need to go to the toilet in the night remember to put them on again (and of course observe the toilet seat procedure outlined elsewhere in this book). If by chance you should drop something, call room service and ask them to vacuum it up for you, and sterilise it before returning.

Telephones

The nest of germs that lives in the mouth and ear pieces of telephones can easily be killed by immersing the handset in a jug of boiling water for ten minutes. The problems come when you have to use other people's apparatus.

I find that a polythene bag filled with disinfectant and concealed in a pocket or handbag is helpful here. It is usually possible to secretly immerse the phone in the disinfectant before use. If it is not and you can do nothing else, hold the receiver at arm's length and shout.

IS MY BRAIN WORKING?

The more intelligent you are the more worries you are likely to have – and the most fundamental worry of an intellectual is of course 'do I exist?' After years puzzling over this definitive problem, and often concluding that I do not exist but am a discarded idea, I have produced the Karamazov Existential Test which quickly and accurately ascertain if the subject does indeed exist.

1. I am.
2. If you can read the above then you do exist.
3. If you can read the above then you really do exist.
4. If you can read the above then you really really do exist.
5. etc.

RADIOACTIVITY

This is really a very misunderstood term so I think I should explain what it really is.

Radioactivity is with us all, everywhere at all times. It consists of tiny particles called electors that split off from radio waves when they are transmitted. Before the wireless there was no radioactivity, now with so many radio stations there is obviously a lot.

'Is It Harmful?' I can almost hear you say at once, and the answer is 'yes' and 'no'. The trouble with Radioactivity is that nine times out of ten you cannot really measure the harm that it causes you (on the tenth time you are dead).

Radioactivity causes you to miss golf balls, to spill ink and to wake up with a hangover. It tends to make you fail exams, lose promotion at work and not be attractive to people of the opposite sex. If you prick yourself while sewing or bang your thumb trying to hit a nail this is due to excess Radioactivity as are all small domestic burns. Splinters, spots and scraping the paintwork on the car are other side effects produced by *fall-out*.

HAEMORRHOIDS

To most people this is an acutely embarrassing problem. It is difficult to talk or write about Haemorrhoids especially to your doctor or chemist. However, there is a code that both these professions understand which does not entail mentioning the actual word or stressing that it feels as if you have a red-hot poker up your bottom.

Your doctor is quite used to dealing with all sorts of personal problems - he has 'seen it all before'. He will probably cough once or twice and ask you how your work is. If you cough back and ask how his work is he will understand you have a delicate subject to discuss. You then need to engage in some version of the following dialogue.

Dr: Is it, er ...?

You: Oh no - well, not exactly.

Dr: But, er, in the old ...?

You: Other end, actually.

Dr: Fine. Take these suppositories twice a day.

Fig. 1.

Fig. 2.

Fig. 3.

If you find the subject too difficult to tackle with your doctor you might try approaching a chemist. Care, however, must be exercised here as coughing and inclining the head will result in a packet of condoms. Try asking for something for some gums and crouching at the same time - this usually achieves the required result.

THE CORRECT WAY TO CUT YOUR NAILS

Cutting toe and finger nails incorrectly is one of the main causes of hospitalisation in the aged. It is worth the time to familiarise yourself with the extent of the problem and how to correct it now, while you are still young, or relatively young (if you can read this you are still relatively young).

Cutting round instead of straight across leads to in-growing toe nails, as we all know. But it is less well-known that the black bits under the ends of your nails are waste matter from inside the body - and therefore dangerous.

Bacteria and other waste matter travels down your limbs and out beneath the nails on your fingers and toes. Here it can easily be transferred into the mouth and hence the bloodstream. It is therefore vital to keep your nails clean and free of this unpleasant debris. Always use children's plastic scissors (to avoid puncturing the skin) and wipe clean with toilet paper as you would for other bodily waste.

TELL-TALE SIGNS TO WATCH OUT FOR

Your pulse is an indication that everything is all right with your body, that your heart is beating and that you are alive. So it is a good idea to take your pulse fairly often.

Surprisingly few people know how to take a pulse properly: you should hold your left wrist very lightly in your right hand wrapping the fingers around it so that the right hand thumb just rests on the knuckles of the left wrist. Do NOT press too hard or this will send the heart into spasm and produce a *phantom pulse*.

Normally you should be able to feel a faint thumping through the veins - about seventy to a hundred thumps a minute is normal, but the more the better. If you do not feel anything do not worry but try again later, your heart can stop beating for quite a while without it mattering much. If you start averaging more 'stops' than 'goes' over a week or so you might be advised to see your physician; it is possible that you are more dead than alive and you are suffering brain damage.

TELEVISIONAIRE'S DISEASE

Description: TD comes in two quite separate strains. Obsessional and Phobic. Both give the hypochondriac plenty to worry about. Of course watching any television is hazardous - cathode ray tubes emit radiation comparable to three Hiroshima bombs (albeit over a period of 120 million years).

In Obsessional TD the patient can do nothing but sit in front of the television soaking up bland programmes by the hour. There is usually a strong inclination towards sub-standard American imports and commercials. Phobic TD often follows Obsessional TD after several years. Here the victim breaks out in a rash at the sight of a TV screen or the mention of a popular programme. It is an unfortunate fact that Phobic TD parents often have Obsessional TD children.

Symptoms: Obsessional TD sufferers can be identified by their hyperactive use of remote control. Desperate to miss no crumb of crass video output, they flick channels at precisely timed intervals so that anyone else in the room has time just to get involved in one programme before it is switched to another.

Phobic TD is more prevalent in the older generations and takes the form of criticising anything on television at all and harping back to the days when the family amused itself around the piano (despite the fact that there are only three people alive in the country who can actually remember doing such a thing - and they were bored to tears).

Treatment: Obsessional TD has to be treated slowly and with care, gradually weaning the patient off the screen, offering attractive substitutes such as sex and large amounts of money. There is no known cure for Phobic TD except allowing the patient to star in his or her own show.

CANCER

People are always asking me how one catches cancer, if it is contagious or hereditary. The sad fact is there is only one way to catch this most debilitating of diseases - reading about it. Cancer was virtually unknown before it started to appear in magazine articles. The simple rule, then, is if you see the word cancer turn the other way. In fact forget you have just read this and you will live long and healthily.

PHOBIAS

A phobia is simply another word for fear, thus a fear of fear could be called a phobia phobia, or fear phobia; a fear of fear phobia is fear phobia phobia or phobia fear phobia or phobia phobia phobia which is quite frightening in itself. Most people suffer from one phobia or another, the most common being Homophobia, fear of other people, and Plexiphobia, fear of things made from plexiglass.

Fortunately modern science, in the form of behavioural psychology, has discovered a very useful strategy for combating virtually any fear. The principle of Behaviourism is to reward positive behaviour while punishing negative behaviour. In the case of phobias this consists of administering cream cakes or sharp blows with a hammer, whichever is appropriate. (Do not attempt this therapy if you suffer from either Cream Cake Phobia, or Hammer Phobia.)

Self-administered behaviour therapy could not be simpler. Below I demonstrate how to rid yourself of Araneina Phobia (fear of spiders).

1. Bring the object of your fear into view, keeping a safe distance.
2. Look at it steadily, trying not to shake, sweat or open your bowels.
3. Squash it with the hammer.
4. Reward yourself with a cream cake.

If your doctor smiles this much he clearly has something to hide.

Either your doctor is finding listening a strain or you have lymph gland problems.

"Just a small incision."

If your doctor looks this pleased it's not because your X-rays are okay - he's just discovered a new and fatal disease.

Your doctor may not be taking you seriously.

Boredom is sometimes difficult to distinguish from deep concentration.

THE WRONG DIAGNOSIS

SYMPTOM: *Pins and Needles*

FIRST DIAGNOSIS: *Nothing to worry about; poor blood circulation due to inactivity.*

REAL PROBLEM: The patient, who lived by the sea, had ingested minute fragments of sand which were circulating in the blood system and had coagulated to form a kind of intravenous sand paper.

SYMPTOM: *Freckles*

FIRST DIAGNOSIS: *Nothing to worry about.*

REAL PROBLEM: Cutaneous dandruff; the freckles are very slow moving spots which are being shed from parts of the body which have brown skin; they will gradually move down the body due to gravity; may herald a variety of illnesses including *Albinism*.

SYMPTOM: *Incontinence*

FIRST DIAGNOSIS: *In younger patients possibly a psychological problem; otherwise an unfortunate symptom of old age - refer to urologist.*

REAL PROBLEM: Patient is unable to spell properly; this could be dyslexia or due to lead poisoning; (patient did not make it to the loo in time which I call *incompetence*).

TELL-TALE SIGNS

What Do I Look For?
Tiny spots or marks at the base of the spine in the middle near your bottom.

What Could They Indicate?
The onset of Legionnaire's Foot, Lockdrawers, Coitus Interruptus, Seasickness, Incontinence.

Isn't It Rather Difficult To See That Bit?
That is why so few people know about it. Use the diagram below to help.

DIY

Description: First discovered after the Second World War when a Mr Arthur G Planstopper tried to build his wife a built-in wardrobe. Although the result was less than happy (it was later turned into a small garage) Mr Planstopper had introduced a disease that was soon to take over most of the Western world. Within a few years quite sane men were putting up shelves, laying drives, renovating sash windows, even digging swimming pools. A large industry grew up to service their needs - giant warehouses full of timber, cement and balking compound.

Symptoms: A pathological desire to ruin property by adding windows, patios, unnecessary furniture and shelves. The complaint usually begins quietly, perhaps a couple of cup hooks or oiling a squeaky door hinge. However, with the slightest encouragement, such as "How clever, darling!" it can quickly progress to full-blown DIY, undertaking such projects as complete re-plumbing or a new roof. The disease usually progresses from the useful to the useless, thus while the early stages can be quite utilitarian terminal cases may be identified by their complete absence of practical use. Typical examples are doors that open at a command and baths that recycle hot water into a series of hot water bottles under mattresses. Apart from the obvious dangers to aesthetic well-being, the patient can endanger the health of all around him.

The progress of the disease may be followed by reference to the Karamazov Tool Chart below. This operates on the notion that the more serious the condition the more unnecessary tools the patient will purchase.

Benign	serious	major	fatal
Hammer Screwdriver Nails Screws	Socket set Spray-gun Level Cement trowel Drill DIY magazines Tile cutter	Hammer attachment Circular saw Electric plane Router Wood lathe	Mortice cutter Metal lathe Oxy-acetylene Asbestos suit Cement mixer Tower crane Dynamite

Treatment: Some specialists claim that removing the patient from the family dwelling can effect a cure - however, recent studies have shown that the complaint is not location specific - the DIYist is quite capable of dismantling a hotel wardrobe just to see how it was put together. Fortunately I have devised a foolproof treatment which, though expensive, is very effective. Give the patient such an enormous task that it will take the rest of his life to complete. Some examples are constructing an orbital motorway around the garden or building a nuclear fallout shelter.

BIRTH

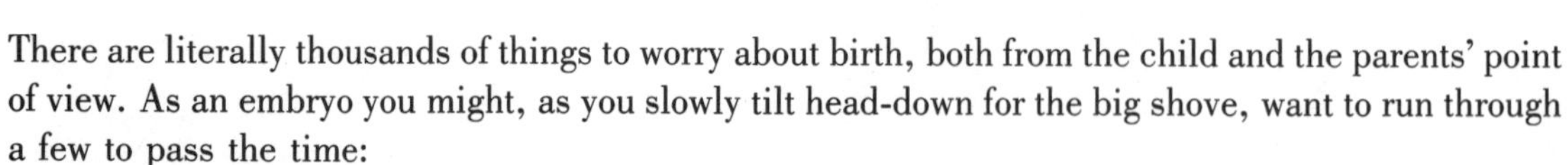

There are literally thousands of things to worry about birth, both from the child and the parents' point of view. As an embryo you might, as you slowly tilt head-down for the big shove, want to run through a few to pass the time:

How the hell am I going to fit through that tiny hole?
Do I want to?
Will it be worth it?
Will I like my mother?
Will she like me?
Will I be breast fed?
Has she been taking pre-natal classes?
Will she continue with the exercises or is she going to embarrass all my friends on the beach with her stretch marks?
Will my father be there?
Is he going to take an equal role in the nurturing process or will I be subjected to a stereotypical, sexist upbringing and have problems with sex the rest of my life?

The parents, of course, have their own concerns:

How the hell is it going to get out of that tiny hole?
Will it have two heads?
Can we afford to feed a baby with two heads?
What will they say at the golf club?
Will it be cleverer than me?
Will it love me?
Will it want to borrow the car and stay out all night?

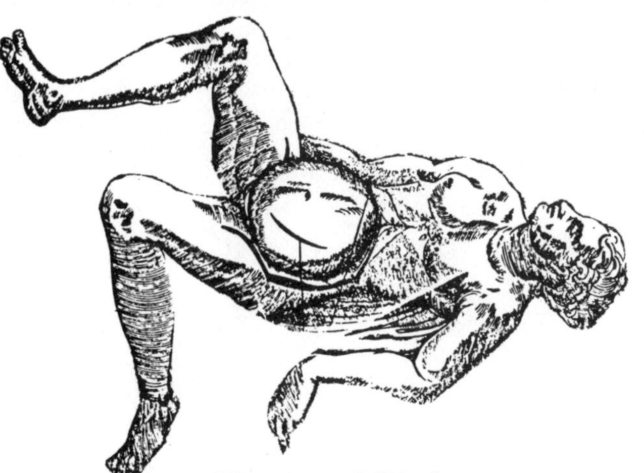

The Actual Birth

Inside the hospital the sister in charge will take you into the labour ward or in a real emergency straight into the delivery room. Don't worry if it all looks a bit strange and sinister to you, the hospital staff know exactly what they are doing and mix-ups very rarely happen. If you are worried check that they have the correct name on the little tag they put round your wrist, though even then they do sometimes get people mixed up and do the wrong thing to them. If you are extra anxious you could ask just which operating theatre you are in and what you are in for. But hospitals these days are very short staffed and the nurses do not usually have the time to answer all your questions.

Now ... what about all those frightening looking machines? Your doctor will not usually be present at the beginning or the end of the birth, or the middle - these days very many operations are directed over the telephone. Who knows, one day soon they may be able to perform everything with robots! So it is best to familiarise yourself in advance with the equipment. The tall machine with lights on top is a Mechanical Dilator, and the smaller one in the corner plugged into a High Voltage socket is a High Voltage Electrical Dilator - which is not as bad as it sounds and very seldom hurts. Beside the bed is the Surgeon's Emergency tray - let's hope he won't need all those needles and knives today! At each end of the bed you will notice straps - these are hardly ever used nowadays. Around the bed you will probably also see two tiers of seats for about thirty to forty people - these are for the students. Without Students today there would be no Doctors tomorrow! And while we are talking about students, do not get too alarmed if your doctor chooses one of them to look after you - he will probably be in constant touch with his secretary by phone.

SLEEPING POSITIONS

The position our bodies take up when we are asleep can be invaluable guides to our general state of health. During sleep the subconscious is free to move the body without the practical limitations of day-to-day life (ie walking, standing etc), and can thus give early-warning signs of impending health problems. Our bodies although asleep are thus trying to tell us something. I first became aware of this when sleeping next to my wife who refused (one useful night) my advances. I did not fly into a rage as I might have done; no, I decided to sit back and watch her sleep. Thank goodness I did! For right there, in front of my eyes, her body revealed to me her deep physiological problem – the woman could not stand me. Several years passed and with more extensive research I was able to devise my Karamazov Sleep Interpretation Charts which are now set to rival Freud's theory on Dreams.

Since it is not easy to note your position when asleep it is best to erect a simple monitoring rig as below. This will provide you with a series of photographs which you can then compare with the diagnostic chart.

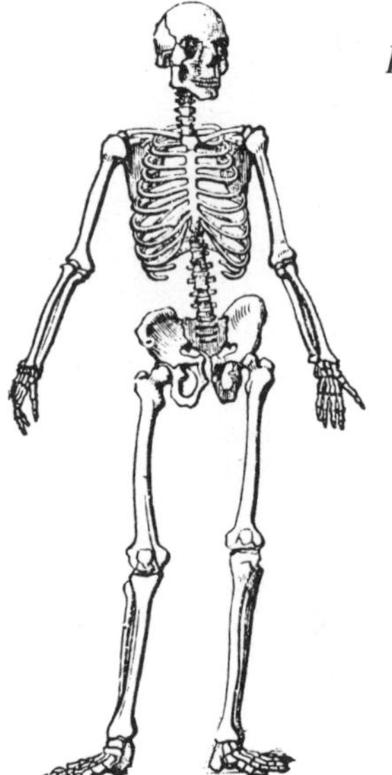

Healthy body asleep

Baghdad Itchy Nose

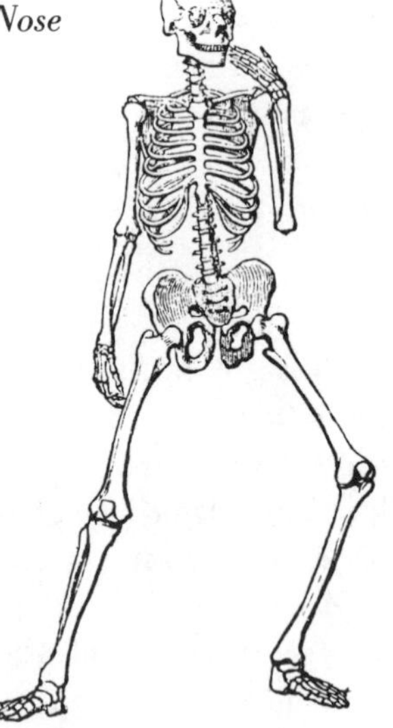

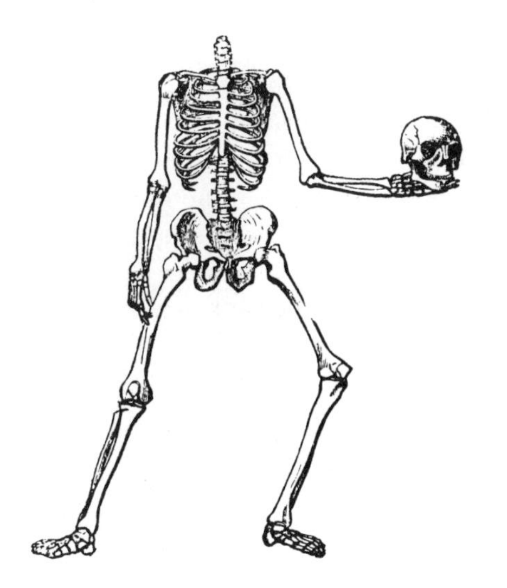

Frustrated person

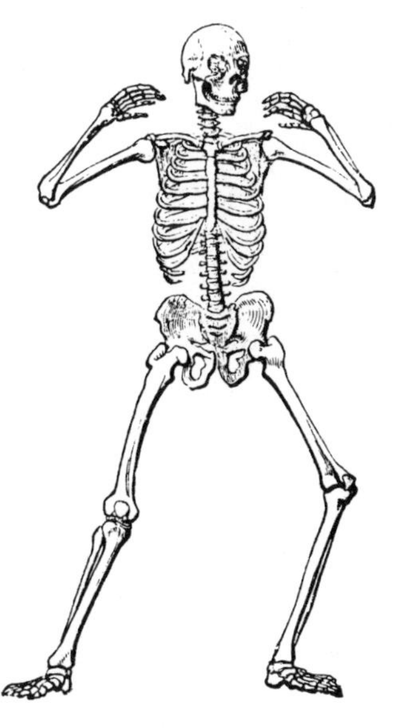

Clear indication of morning sickness

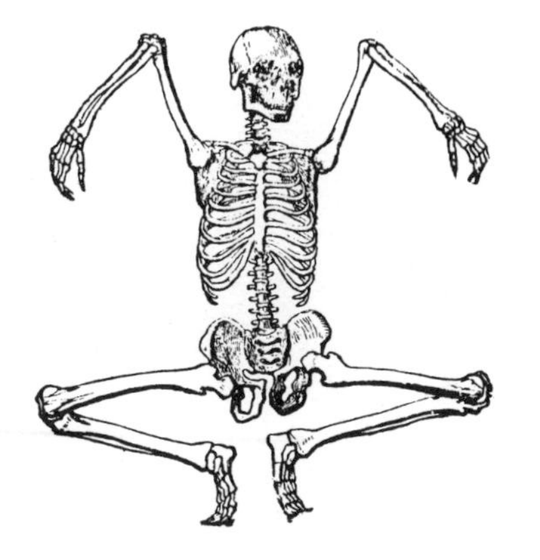

Serious sleeping problems

HYPOCHONDRIAC TRANSFERENCE

This intriguing phenomenon forms the cornerstone of Karamazov Hypochondriacanalysis*. I first discovered the effect while working with a group of hypochondriacs in a fashionable suburb of Vienna (near Leeds). As I worked on the patients, all of whom were suffering from delusions of grandeur, I was gratified to notice that their symptoms were gradually disappearing - a Mr. Nietberger, who had previously insisted he was the Messiah now reverted to being a greengrocer; a bought ledger clerk no longer claimed to be Bernard Shaw and even the local butcher, a convincing Norman Tebbit, returned to his less harmful occupation. However, just as my patients recovered so I found myself taking on their afflictions and by the end of the eight sessions I was a preaching playwright determined to cut back public sector spending. Fortunately I was able to off-load these onto an unsuspecting group of visiting Japanese professors.

In this way then, was discovered the Theory of Hypochondriac Transference. The principle of the phenomenon is simple - a hypochondriac with any given real or imagined problem can, simply by talking about it, transfer the worry to another party. Thus the sufferer of chronic piles can unload his fears onto anyone who is prepared to listen. Simply stroll up to the chosen Transferee and relate the symptoms of the complaint. Within ten minutes they will make some excuse, slip off to the bathroom and start desperately checking themselves.

The hypochondriac can then walk off, lightened by the knowledge that at least one other person is suffering similar torment.

*Any claims to the contrary, especially by my colleague and ex co-researcher E.R. Young (pronounced Young) can be discounted - the aforementioned gentleman is the unfortunate victim of pathological jealousy.

POSTURE

Nearly everyone at one time or another suffers from back-pain - this is because our spine was designed to be used horizontally. However, except for some rare, though quite exciting occasions, crawling on all fours is not socially acceptable. In order to gain attention and sympathy the hypochondriac must adopt the correct posture.

Karamazov Posture

The Karamazov Technique of Correct Posture is based on two simple exercises to achieve the necessary curvature of the spine. First, suspend yourself from a meat-hook placed between the shoulder blades; for parties and other social gatherings the rope may be disguised as a plant.

The second exercise should be done each morning. Place three heavy volumes (preferably of a worrying nature) on the back of the neck and walk with hunched shoulders for twenty-five minutes.

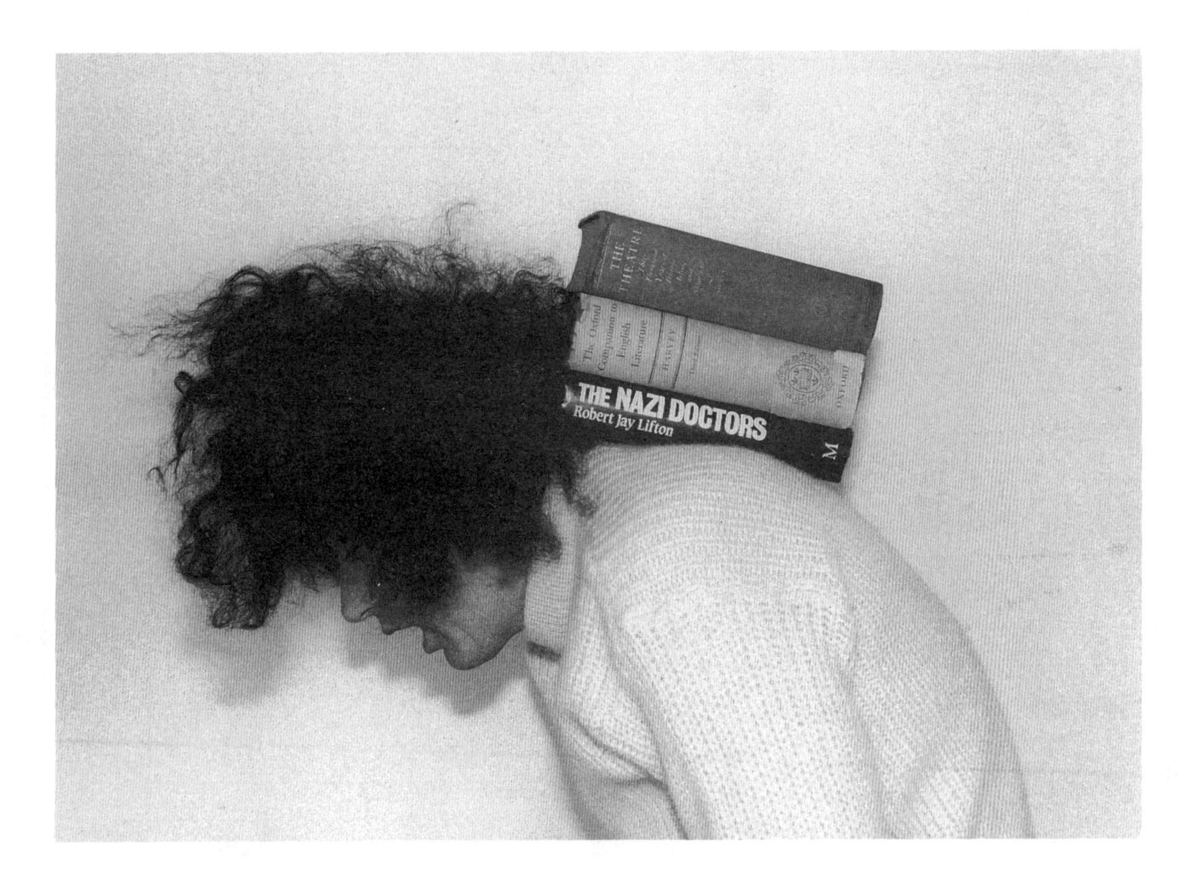

ARE GETTING

These days public awareness of the need to eat properly, get the right vitamins, go to the toilet regularly, take plenty of exercise, refrain from sex etc, is so high that it may seem silly to even mention these as topics.

Deficiency

Symptom:	Vitamin C	Calcium	Intercourse	Dirty Jokes	Vitamin E	Alcohol	Exercise	Doctors	Sex	Food
Frequent Motions				●			●			
Dizziness			●							
Spots Before Eyes	●									
Small Tits								●		
Loose Stools										●
Rapid Heart Beats									●	
Small Pupils		●								
Overweight					●					
Itchy Groin									●	
Palpitations						●				
Flakey Skin	●									
Big Erection			●							
Painting Spells										●
Trembling									●	
Shaking Limbs								●		
Watery Eyes					●					
Itchy Scalp		●								
Stomach Ache				●						
Nausea							●			
Runny Nose										
Persistent Cough						●				
Falling Over									●	
The Shits					●					
Wanting To Stay in Bed			●							
Feeling Randy						●				
Sneezing	●									
Kidney Pains				●					●	
Headaches								●		
Sounds in Ears					●					
One Leg shorter than other										●
No Heart Beat										

YOU ENOUGH?

Nevertheless, even in civilised twentieth century society people get deficiencies. If you feel that you may not be getting enough of something check your symptoms with the chart here.

Excess

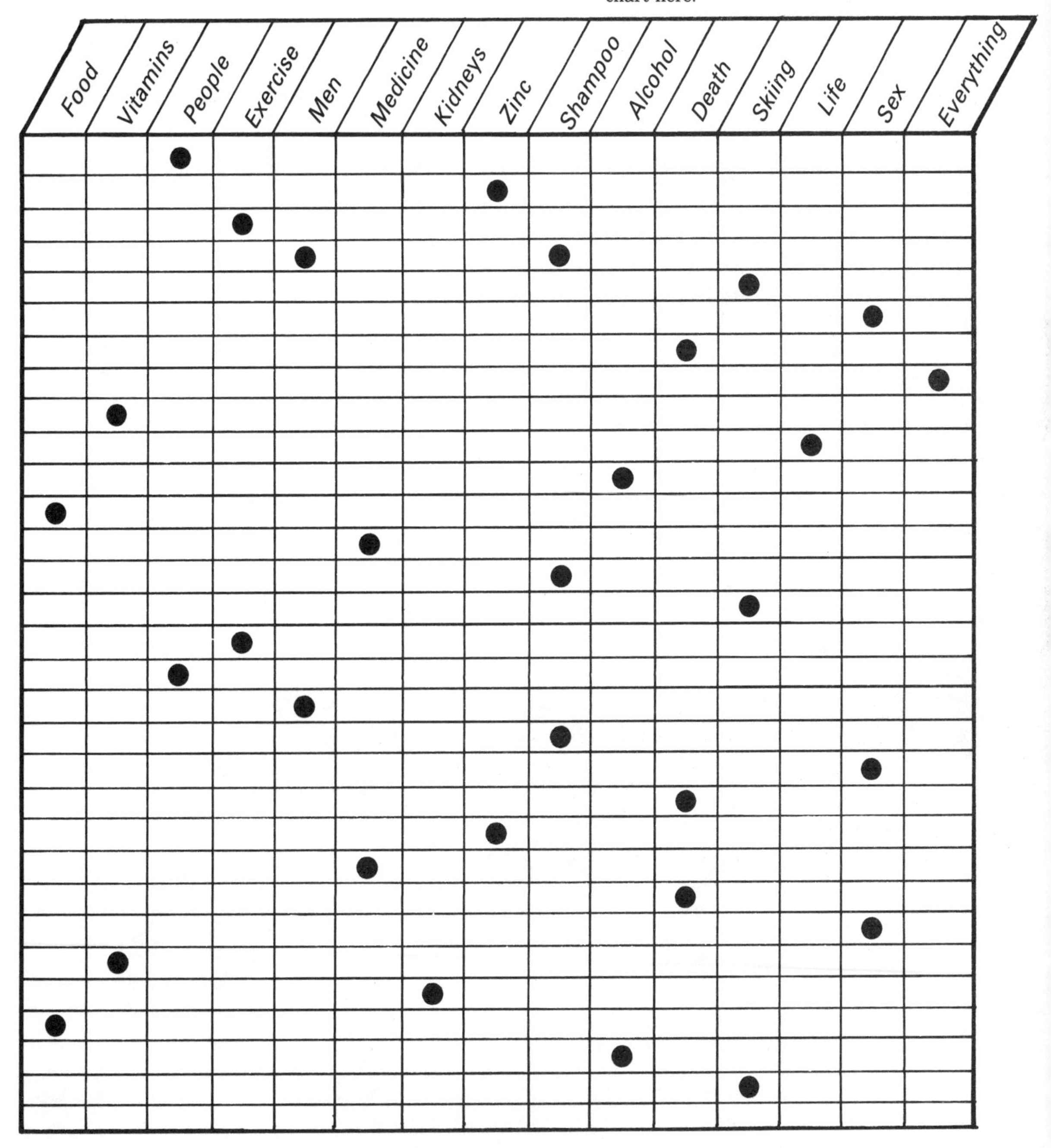

STRESS

As we all know one of the most common causes of cardiac arrest is stress. What is less well-known is that most stress is caused by worrying about stress. The incidence of stress related diseases (angina, strokes and shouting) has increased in direct proportion to the press coverage of the subject. One possible solution, therefore, to this modern plague is simply to stop reading newspapers and magazines. However, this can lead to intense withdrawal symptoms and an outbreak of Media Missingitis, where the patient is convinced that in the one paper he has not read or the TV show he missed was information vital to his continuing existence on the planet.

A simpler solution is my Relaxation Technique, developed in conjunction with the Hungarian Light Cheese Board. The first step in reducing tension is to ascertain the areas of highest stress. I have therefore designed a brief questionnaire to pin-point these trouble-spots.

1. Your lover of five years tells you they have been having an affair with your best friend for the last four years and eight months. Do you:

   a) Remain calm and suggest you all go on holiday to talk about it.
   b) Fall asleep.
   c) Reach for the bread knife.
   d) Sit very quietly feeling as if someone is pumping you up with a bicycle pump.

2. You are thirty minutes late for a vital business meeting, stuck in a five-mile tail-back, it's 85° and you're wearing thermal underwear. Do you:

   a) Wind down the window and have a chat with the car next to you.
   b) Read a book.
   c) Hum a little tune.
   d) Explode.

3. Your five year old child did not come back after school. It is now after midnight and there has been a rash of child-molesters in the neighbourhood. Do you:

   a) Think it'll be a formative experience.
   b) Leave the back door open and go to bed.
   c) Have a bath.
   d) Get your bazooka out.

4. You have just completed a questionnaire. Were you:

   a) Quite interested.
   b) Not bothered.
   c) Keen to do well.
   d) Paralysed with fear.

Results: whatever you answered you really wanted to answer (d) to everything – this means you are highly stressed and will probably die soon unless you learn to relax.

Relaxation

1. Sit comfortably in a chair or lie on a bed.
2. Relax.

For some people, simply reading the word STRESS can cause palpitations; especially when it is written like this ...**STRESS** ... or even like this ... **STRESS** ... Stress can be brought on by a number of things, mainly by reading words like **CORONARY** or **HEART FAILURE**. The sight of a graph has been known to bring on this condition as has the words **BLOOD PRESSURE** or the sound of medical equipment going bleep.

Examine these three Stress Graphs:

1. The Wadsworth Analyser

2. The Woolf Accumulator

3. The McGowan Exponential Curve

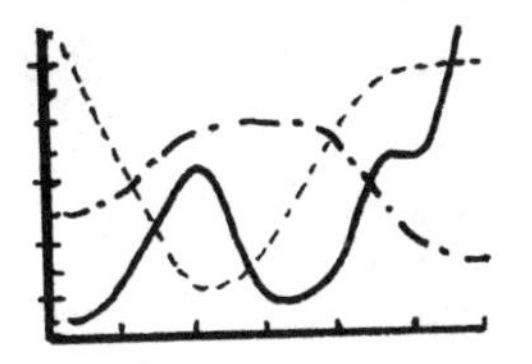

Which graph did you find the most stressful to examine?

NASTY SKIN DISORDERS

ARROWS

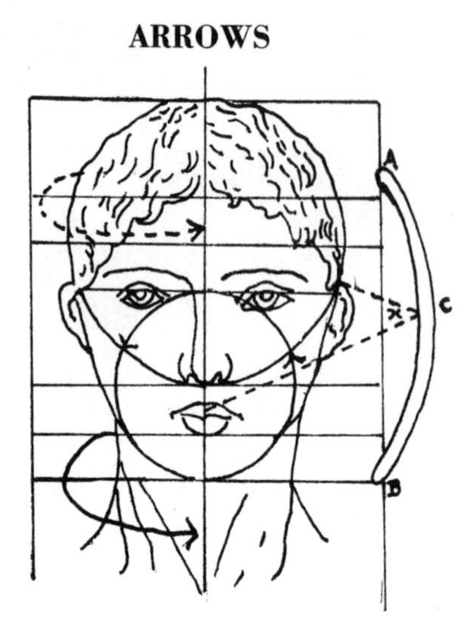

An unpleasantly infectious disease. It can become difficult to be taken seriously as anything other than a medical illustration.

BLOTCHY BLEMISHES

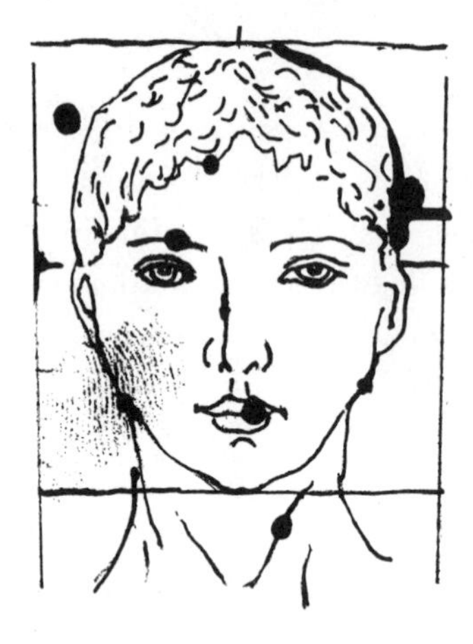

Caused by ink clotting.

OFF-SET PRINTING

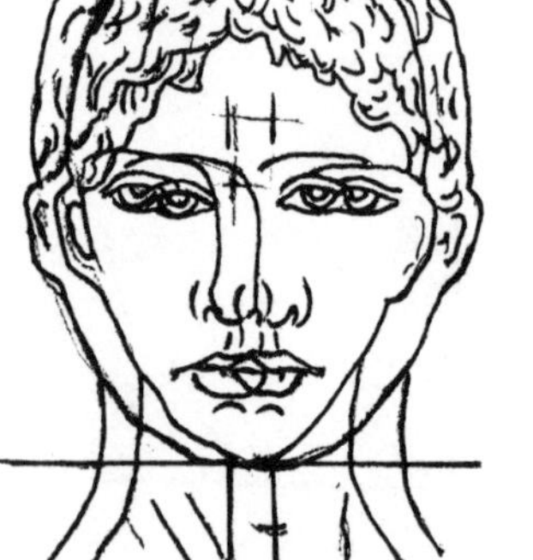

A nasty double edge can develop along your profile.

Easily caused by a careless graphic artist.

SKIN GRAIN

Wooden appearance by over-enlargement.

DR. KARAMAZOV'S EYE TEST

IT IS A WELL DOCUM
ENTED MEDICAL FACT
THAT THE HUMAN EYE CAN
RAPIDLY ADJUST FROM FOCUSSIN
G ON VERY LARGE OBJECTS TO FOCUSSI
NG ON VERY SMALL ONES, HOWEVER, MY
RESEARCHES HAVE CONCLUSIVELY SHOWN
THAT SUCH ACTION CAN PERMANENTLY DAMAGE
THE EYESIGHT

THE WRONG DIAGNOSIS

SYMPTOM: *Frog in Throat*

FIRST DIAGNOSIS: *Hoarseness due to sore larynx; aftermath of laryngitis.*

REAL PROBLEM: A frog in the throat; spawn can be deposited in water reservoirs by herons and other birds; the water is then siphoned off into the domestic water supply.

FLUORINE AND YOU

You have probably read and heard quite a lot about the Government putting fluorine in the water and, now, in the electricity supply. I will not go into the morals of this issue in a medical text book but describe what happens in a scientific manner.

Fluorine is a white pastey substance which comes in tubes, generally about 4 to 8 inches long (10 to 20 cm). Sometimes fluorine is just white and sometimes it has red stripes in it; in most cases it tastes of peppermint.

Clearly it would not be economic for the Government to use millions of tubes of fluorine from Safeway, so when they want to insert it into the water or electricity supply they buy giant economy size tubes.

Why Put Fluorine In The Electricity Supply?

The Government claims that the success that it has had with reducing dental cavities by putting fluorine in the water has outweighed the disadvantages many times. Putting fluorine in the electricity supply will, it is anticipated, halve the number of winter flu victims.

How Will It Affect Me?

You should not notice anything very much other than perhaps that your television or washing machine may smell slightly of peppermint.

Are There Any Long Term Effects?

Yes - but it is hoped that these will be good ones. Flu should halve, and a useful spin off should be that electrical appliances will not get decay.

What Else Are They Going To Put In Things?

There are currently plans to put Vitamin C in the gas system.

IS MY BRIAN WORKING?

Another of the tell-tale signs that all may not be well up top is loss of concentration. You may find yourself reading the same sentence more than once. You may find yourself reading the same sentence more than once. It is difficult to scientifically measure this sort of

There are some qualitative tests that can help. These should be administered by a psychologist but in

If you cannot manage all the tests do not worry; plenty of people who

Start at the beginning and time yourself while

a)
b)
c)
d)
e)
f)
g)

Answers: 4) 6) 1) 5) 3) 2) 7)

HEADSTONES

Sadly there are many diseases associated with old age, Tedium nervosa, Baldstones, Prostrate, Vile Duct Blockage, Pre-Senile Dementia etc and Headstones. All of these are diseases linked to the ageing process. While none of these others is usually fatal, Headstones always is.

What Are The Symptoms?
Sometimes brought on by an attack of Prostrate, Headstones are usually squarish in shape, cold and fairly heavy.

What Is The Treatment?
There is really very little that medical science can do about them at the moment. Probably the best advice is to avoid them for as long as possible.

Are They Always Fatal?

Yes. Very.

HYPOCHONDRIAC'S CARD

To be carried with you at all times.

I am not dead – just seriously ill. I do not wish any of my organs to be removed without my verbal consent.

Call a doctor – do NOT attempt First Aid.

Please use latex gloves in inside jacket pocket when touching me.